2ND EDITION / EASY PIANO

S0-BKE-148

Disney
Mega-Hit Movies

ISBN 978-0-634-04514-1

WALT DISNEY MUSIC COMPANY
WONDERLAND MUSIC COMPANY, INC.

DISTRIBUTED BY

HAL•LEONARD®
CORPORATION

7777 W. BLUEMOUND RD. P.O. BOX 13819 MILWAUKEE, WI 53213

In Australia Contact:
Hal Leonard Australia Pty. Ltd.
4 Lentara Court
Cheltenham, Victoria, 3192 Australia
Email: ausadmin@halleonard.com.au

Visit Hal Leonard Online at
www.halleonard.com

CONTENTS

3 **BE OUR GUEST**
Beauty and the Beast

18 **BEAUTY AND THE BEAST**
Beauty and the Beast

26 **BELLE**
Beauty and the Beast

40 **CAN YOU FEEL THE LOVE TONIGHT**
The Lion King

23 **CIRCLE OF LIFE**
The Lion King

48 **COLORS OF THE WIND**
Pocahontas

62 **FRIEND LIKE ME**
Aladdin

72 **GO THE DISTANCE**
Hercules

78 **GOD HELP THE OUTCASTS**
The Hunchback of Notre Dame

53 **HAKUNA MATATA**
The Lion King

84 **HAWAIIAN ROLLER COASTER RIDE**
Lilo & Stitch

90 **I JUST CAN'T WAIT TO BE KING**
The Lion King

100 **IF I DIDN'T HAVE YOU**
Monsters, Inc.

112 **IF I NEVER KNEW YOU (LOVE THEME
FROM POCAHONTAS)**
Pocahontas

107 **THE INCREDITS**
The Incredibles

120 **JUST AROUND THE RIVERBEND**
Pocahontas

126 **KISS THE GIRL**
The Little Mermaid

138 **LES POISSONS**
The Little Mermaid

144 **LOOK THROUGH MY EYES**
Brother Bear

133 **THE MEDALLION CALLS**
Pirates of the Caribbean:
The Curse of the Black Pearl

152 **MY FUNNY FRIEND AND ME**
The Emperor's New Groove

170 **ONE JUMP AHEAD**
Aladdin

180 **OUR TOWN**
Cars

161 **PART OF YOUR WORLD**
The Little Mermaid

188 **REFLECTION**
Mulan

198 **SOMEDAY**
The Hunchback of Notre Dame

204 **THAT'S HOW YOU KNOW**
Enchanted

214 **TRUE LOVE'S KISS**
Enchanted

193 **TWO WORLDS**
Tarzan™

220 **UNDER THE SEA**
The Little Mermaid

234 **WE'RE ALL IN THIS TOGETHER**
High School Musical

229 **WHAT I'VE BEEN LOOKING FOR**
High School Musical

240 **WHEN SHE LOVED ME**
Toy Story 2

245 **A WHOLE NEW WORLD**
Aladdin

252 **YOU ARE THE MUSIC IN ME**
High School Musical 2

274 **YOU'LL BE IN MY HEART (POP VERSION)**
Tarzan™

260 **YOU'VE GOT A FRIEND IN ME**
Toy Story

264 **ZERO TO HERO**
Hercules

BE OUR GUEST

from Walt Disney's BEAUTY AND THE BEAST

Lyrics by HOWARD ASHMAN
Music by ALAN MENKEN

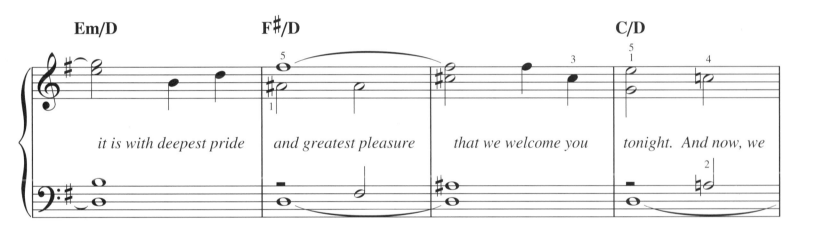

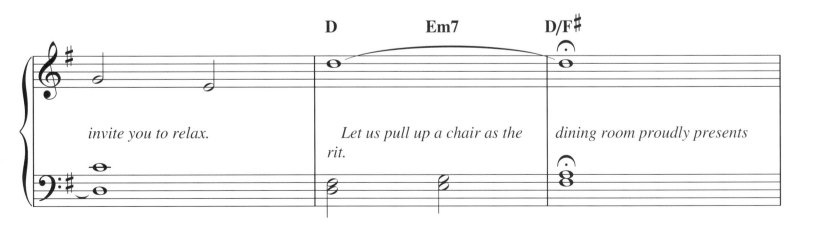

4

your dinner! Be our guest! Be our guest! Put our

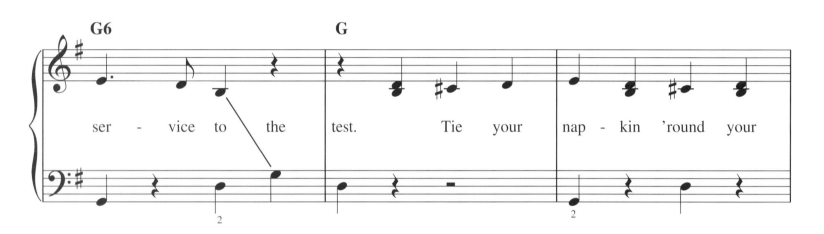

ser - vice to the test. Tie your nap - kin 'round your

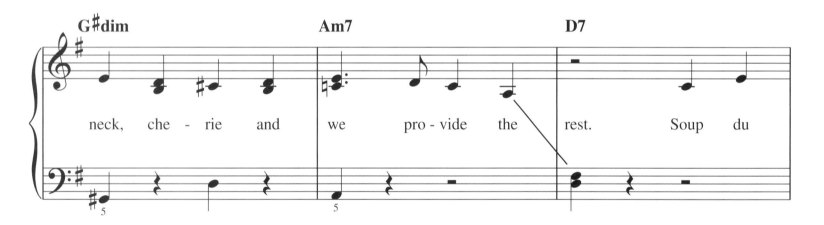

neck, che - rie and we pro - vide the rest. Soup du

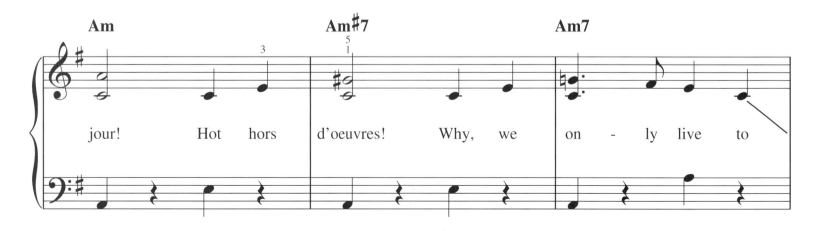

jour! Hot hors d'oeuvres! Why, we on - ly live to

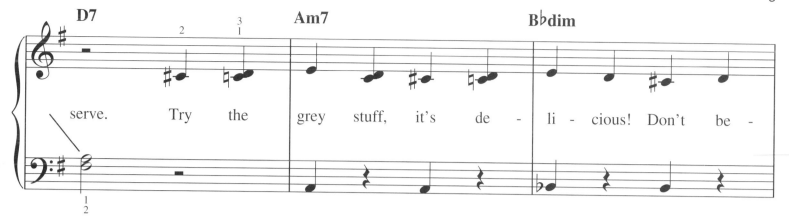

serve. Try the grey stuff, it's de - li - cious! Don't be -

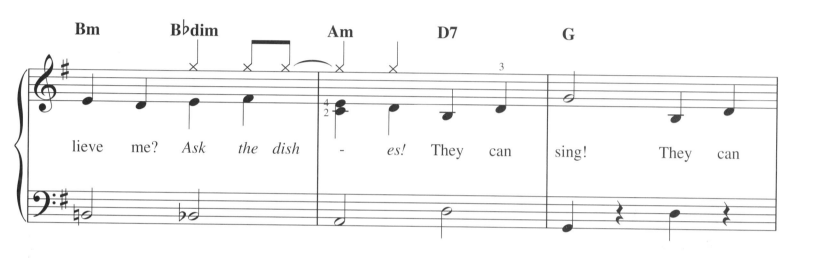

lieve me? *Ask the dish* - *es!* They can sing! They can

dance! *Af - ter all,* *Miss, this is* *France!* And a

din - ner here is nev - er sec - ond best.

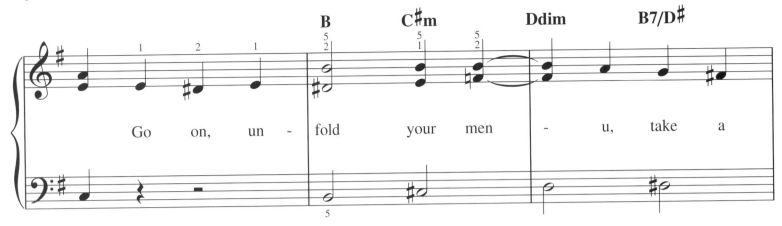

Go on, un - fold your men - u, take a

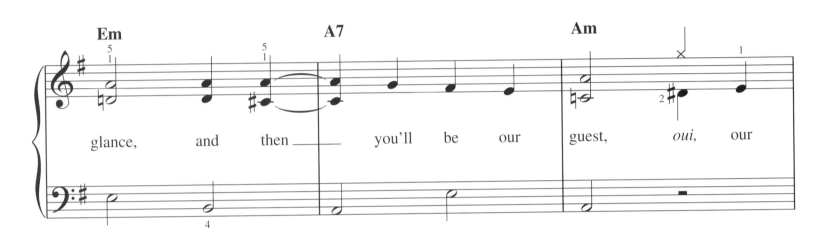

glance, and then _____ you'll be our guest, *oui*, our

guest! Be our guest! Beef ra - gout! Cheese souf -

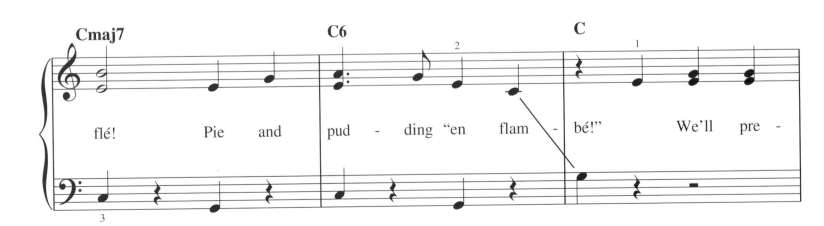

flé! Pie and pud - ding "en flam - bé!" We'll pre -

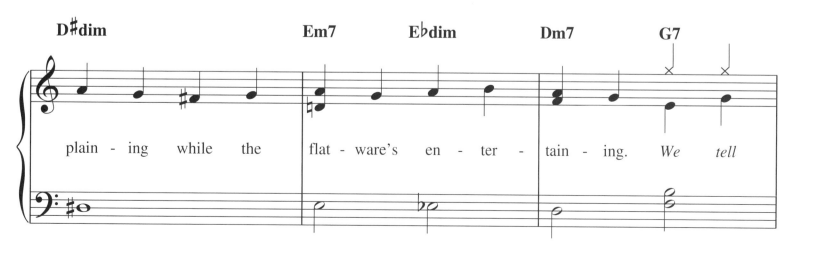

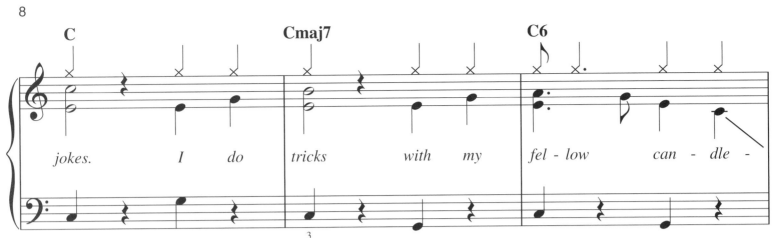

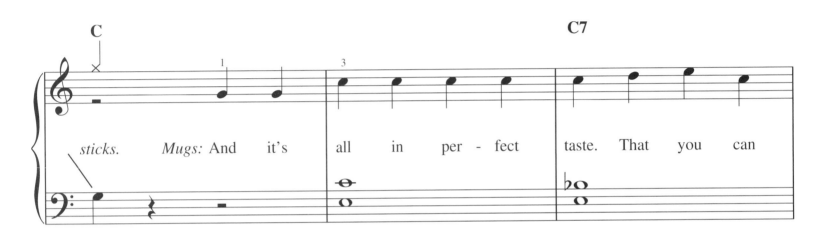

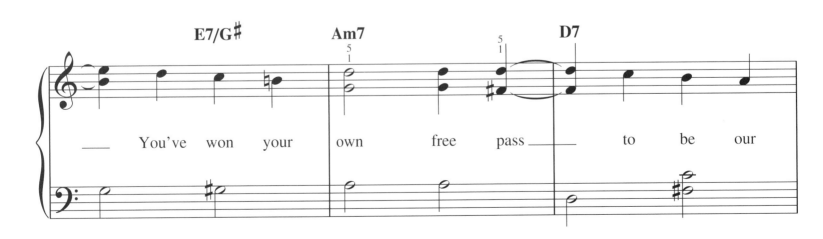

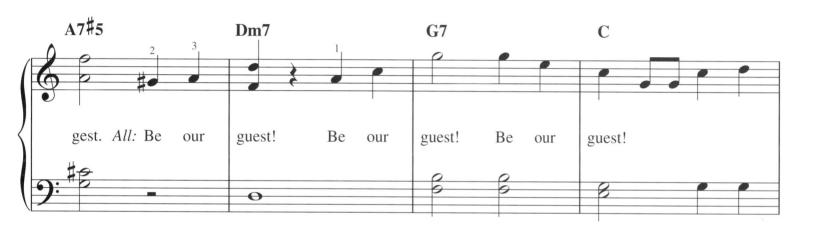

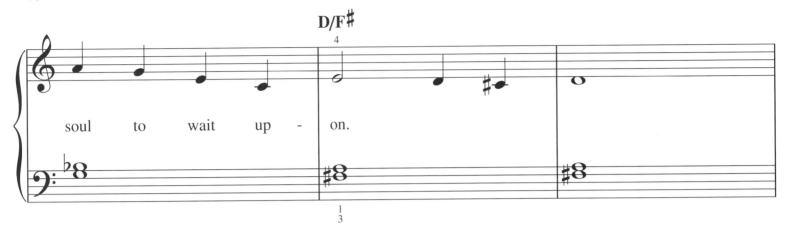

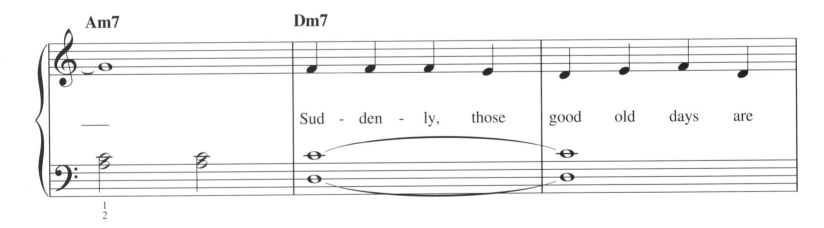

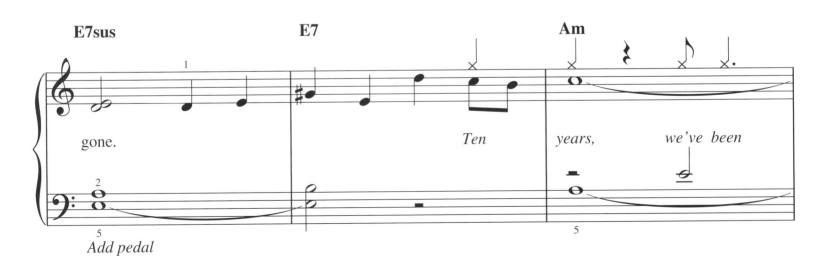

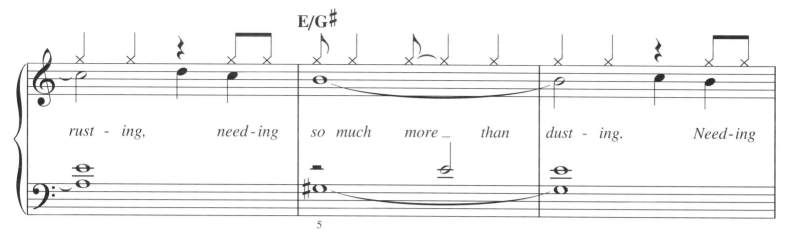

rust - ing, need-ing so much more __ than dust - ing. Need-ing

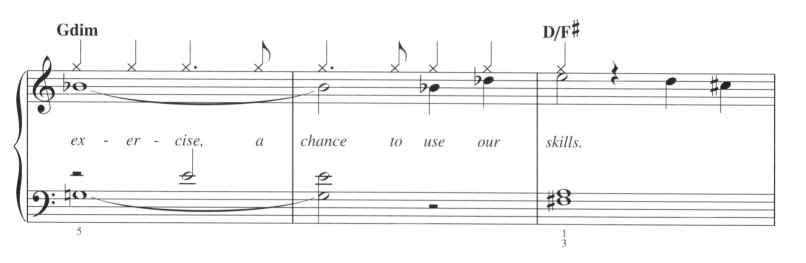

ex - er - cise, a chance to use our skills.

Most days, we just lay a - round the

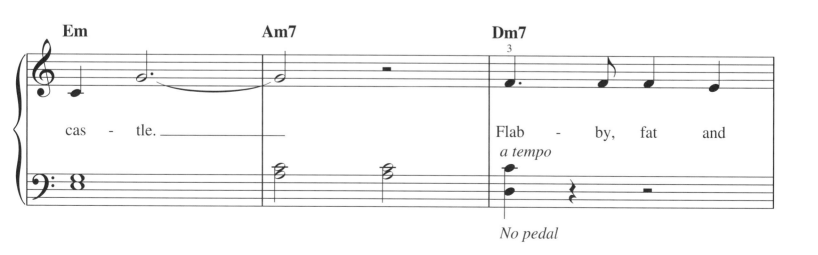

cas - tle. _____ Flab - by, fat and

la - zy. You walked in *and oops - a - dai - sy! Mrs. Potts:* It's a

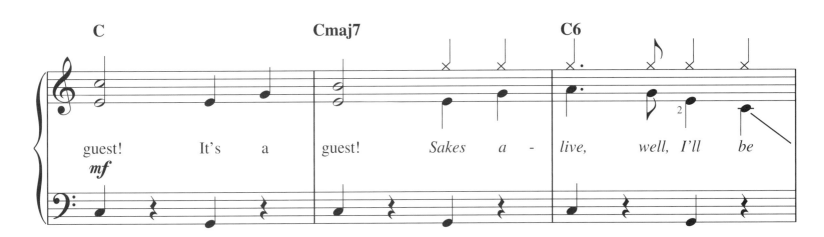

guest! It's a guest! *Sakes a - live, well, I'll be*

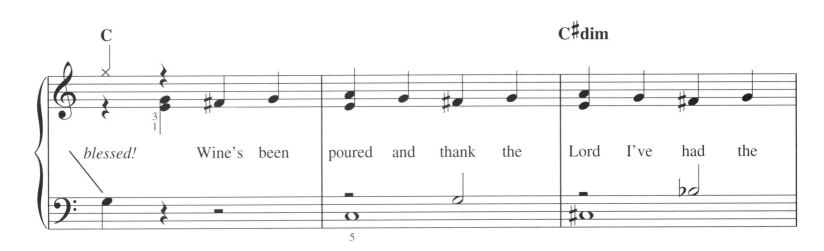

blessed! Wine's been poured and thank the Lord I've had the

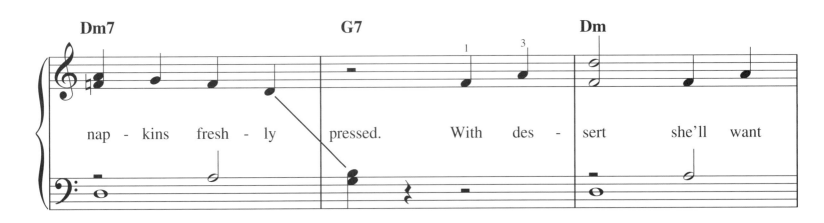

nap - kins fresh - ly pressed. With des - sert she'll want

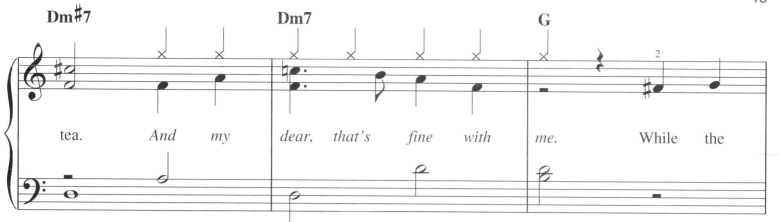

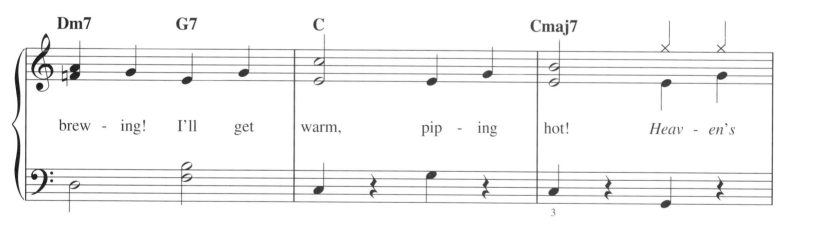

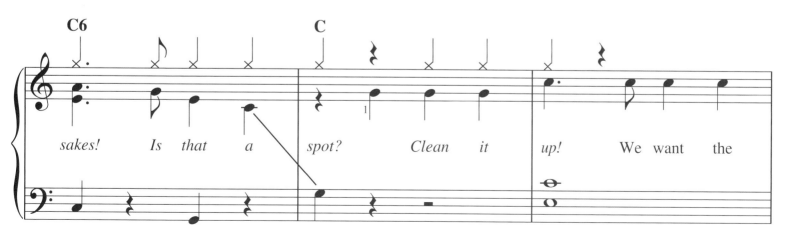

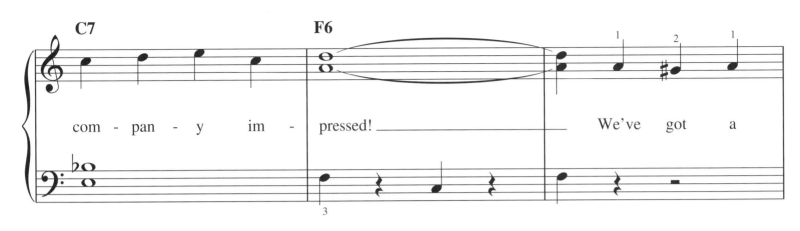

com - pan - y im - pressed! _____ We've got a

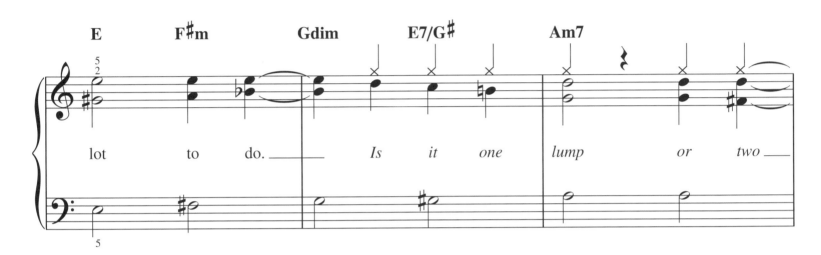

lot to do. ___ *Is it one lump or two* ___

___ *for you, our* *guest? Chorus:* She's our guest! *Mrs. Potts:* She's our

guest! *Chorus:* She's our guest! Be our guest! Be our

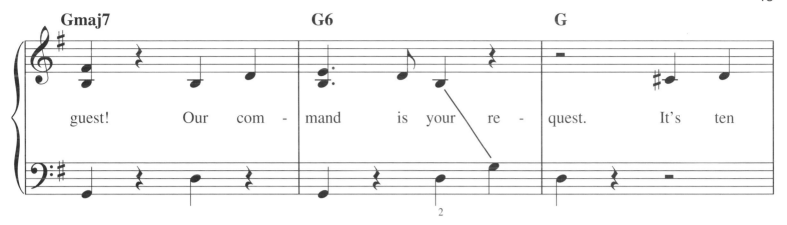

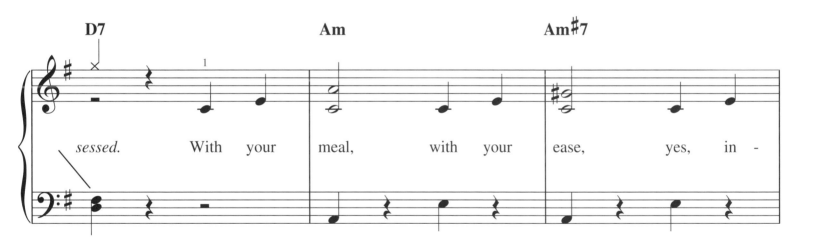

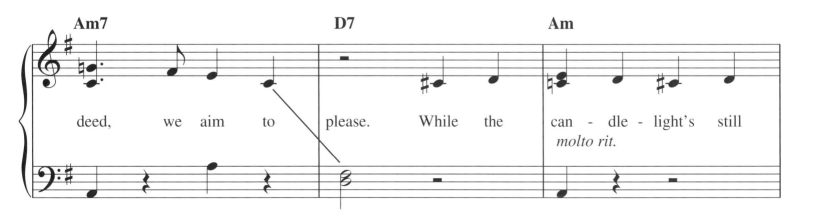

D7   **G7**

glow - ing let us help you, we'll keep go - ing course by

rit.

Much slower

C   **Cmaj7**   **C6**

course, one by one! 'Til you shout, "E - nough. I'm

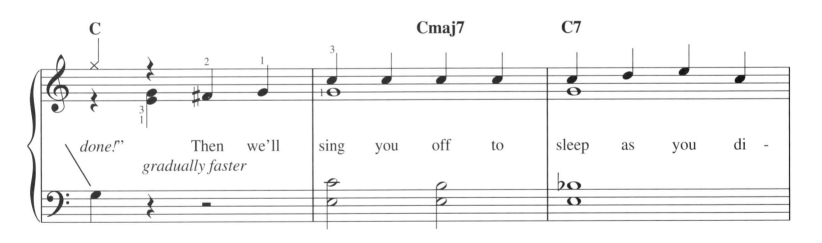

C   **Cmaj7**   **C7**

done!" Then we'll sing you off to sleep as you di -

gradually faster

F6   **E**   **F#m7**

gest. To - night you'll prop your feet ___

a tempo

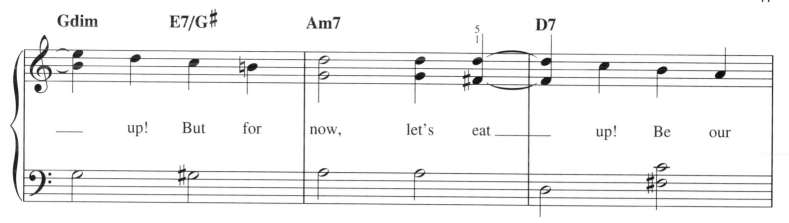

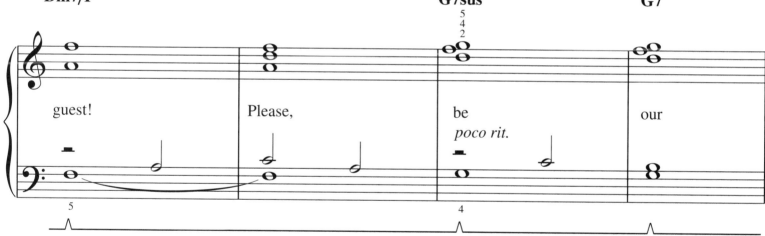

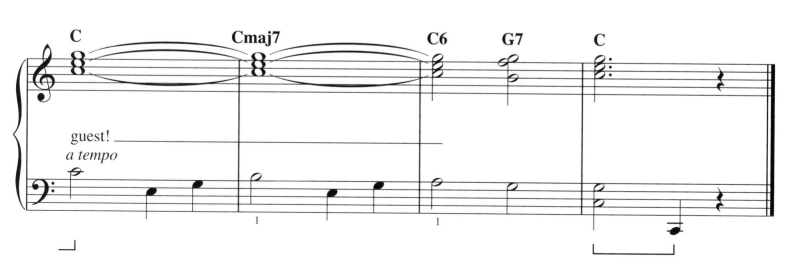

BEAUTY AND THE BEAST

from Walt Disney's BEAUTY AND THE BEAST

Lyrics by HOWARD ASHMAN
Music by ALAN MENKEN

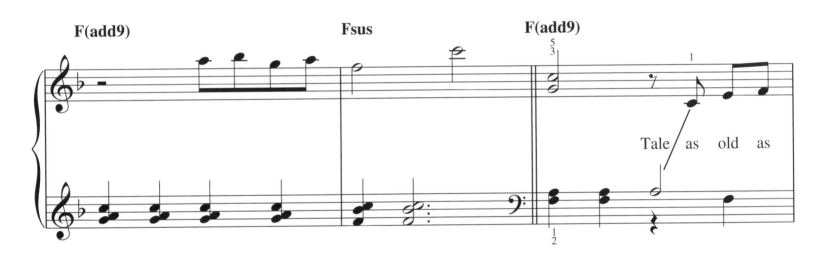

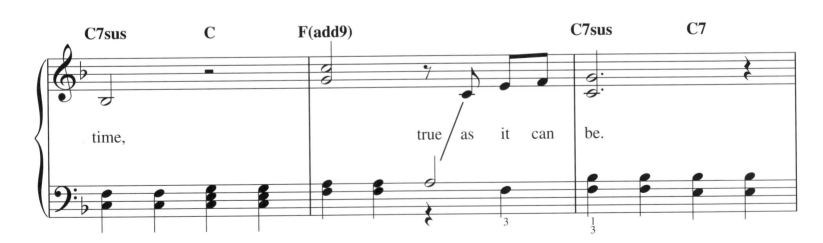

F(add9)   Am

Bare - ly e - ven friends, then some - bod - y

C7sus   F(add9)

bends un - ex - pect - ed - ly.   Just a lit - tle

C7sus C F(add9)   Cm7 F7

change.   Small, to say the least. Both a lit - tle

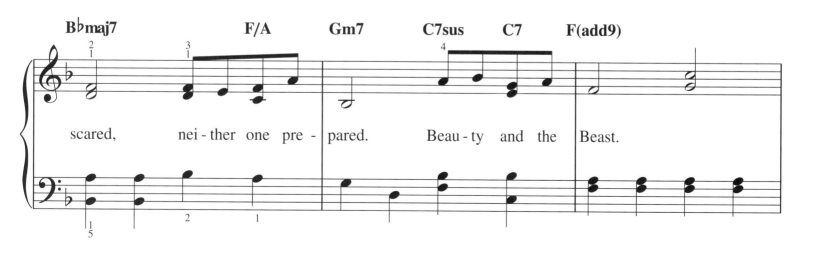

B♭maj7   F/A Gm7 C7sus C7 F(add9)

scared, nei - ther one pre - pared. Beau - ty and the Beast.

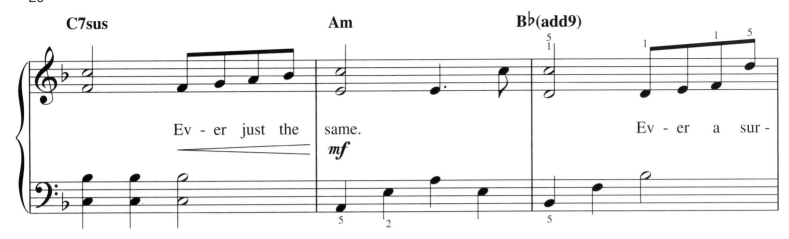

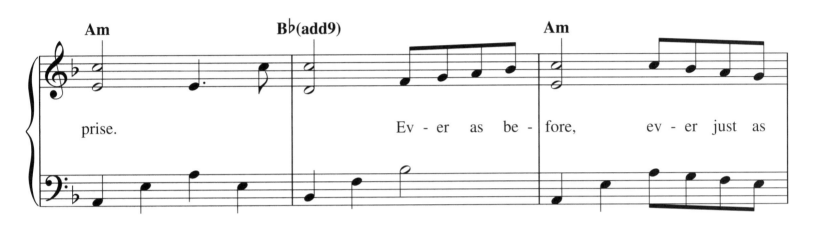

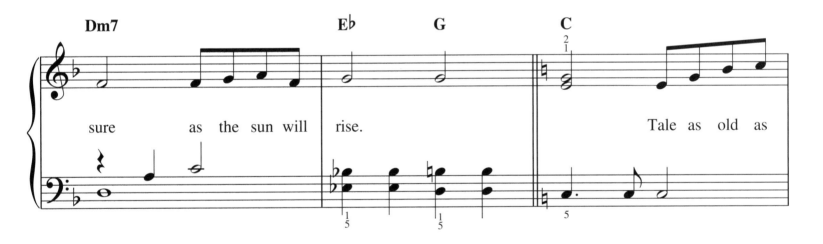

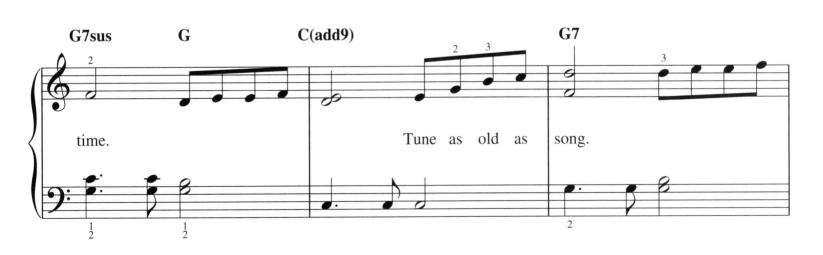

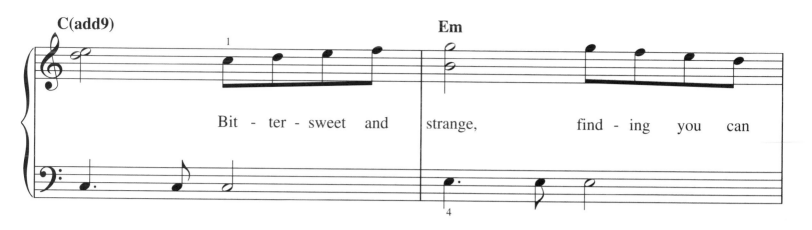

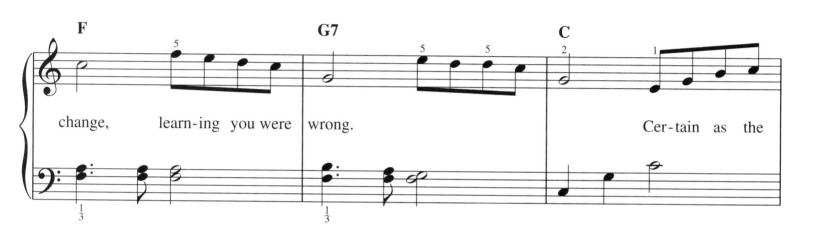

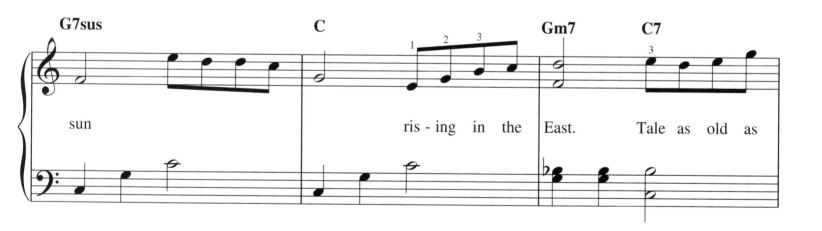

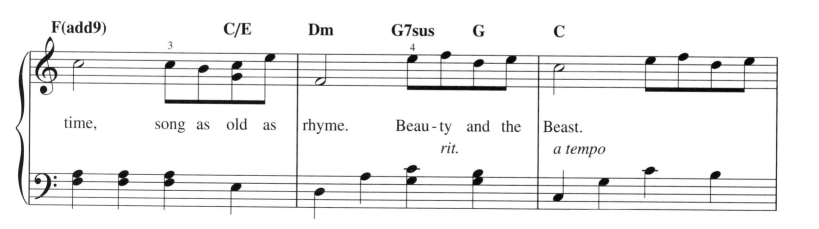

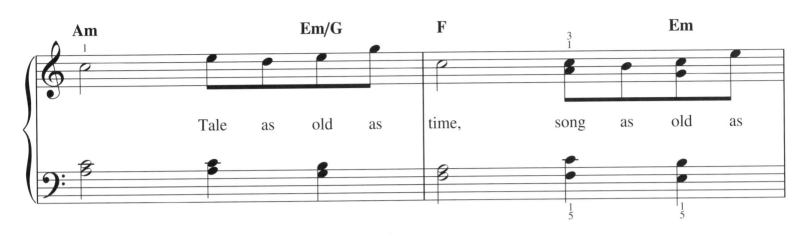

Tale as old as time, song as old as

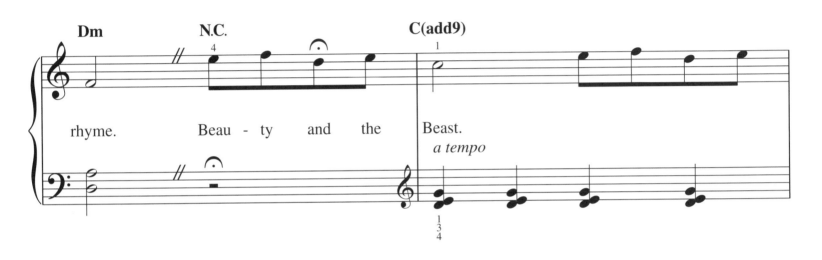

rhyme. Beau - ty and the Beast.

a tempo

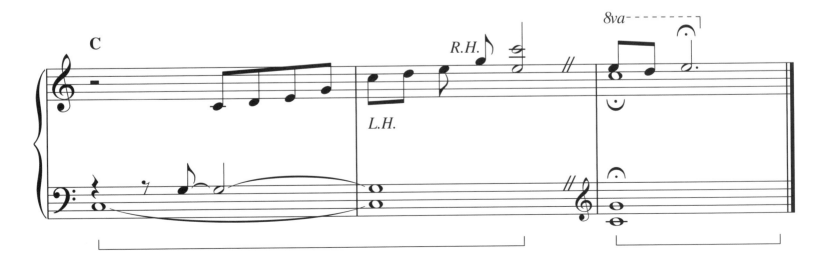

CIRCLE OF LIFE
from Walt Disney Pictures' THE LION KING

Music by ELTON JOHN
Lyrics by TIM RICE

24

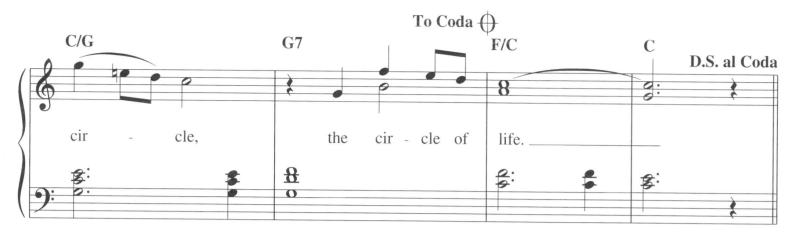

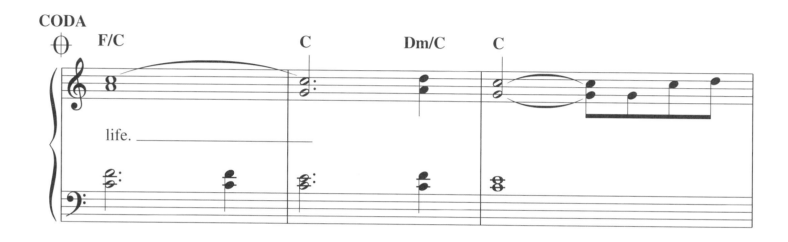

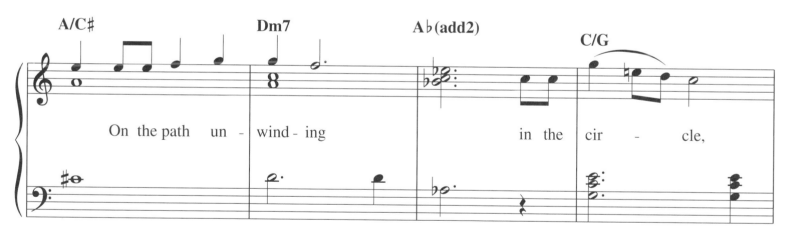

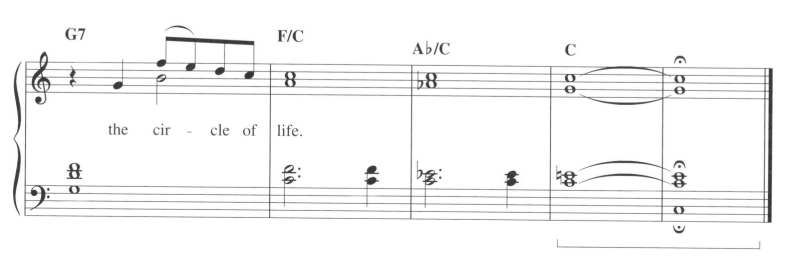

BELLE
from Walt Disney's BEAUTY AND THE BEAST

Lyrics by HOWARD ASHMAN
Music by ALAN MENKEN

jour!   Bon - *jour!* Bon - *jour!* Bon - *jour!*

Belle: There goes the bak - er with his tray, like
Townsfolk: Look there she goes that girl is strange, like no
Townsfolk: Look there she goes that girl is so pe -

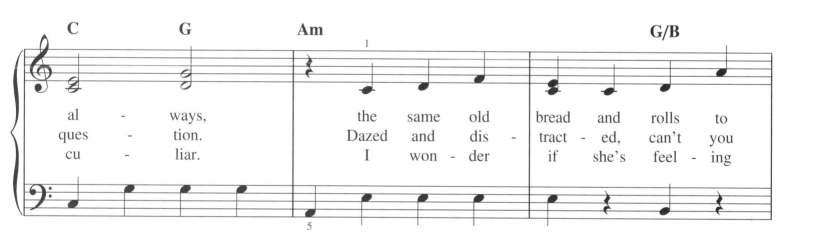

al - ways, the same old bread and rolls to
ques - tion. Dazed and dis - tract - ed, can't you
cu - liar. I won - der if she's feel - ing

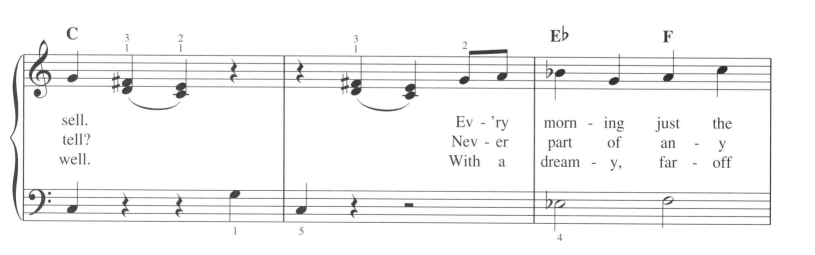

sell. Ev - 'ry morn - ing just the
tell? Nev - er part of an - y
well. With a dream - y, far - off

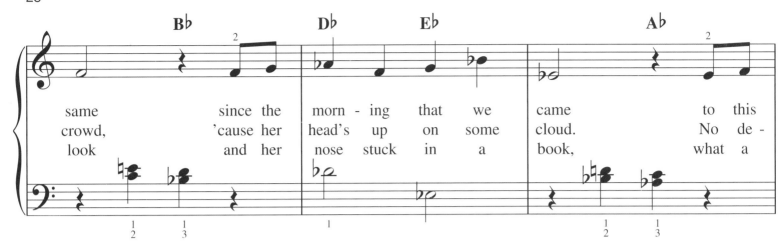

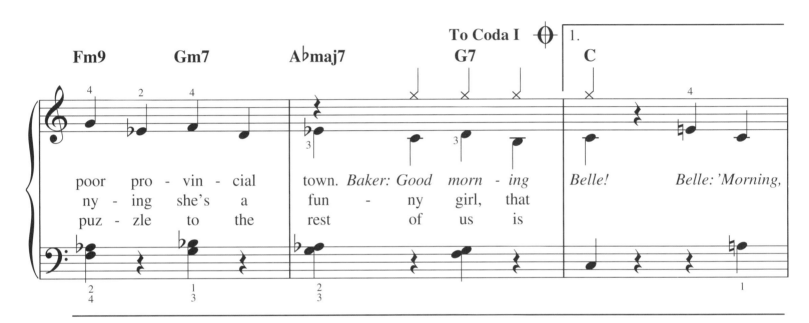

rie! *The* baguettes! Hurry up! | Belle.

Man I: Bon-jour. | *Woman I:* Good day. | *Man I:* How is your

fam-'ly? | *Woman II:* Bon-jour. | *Man II:* Good day. | *Woman II:* How is your

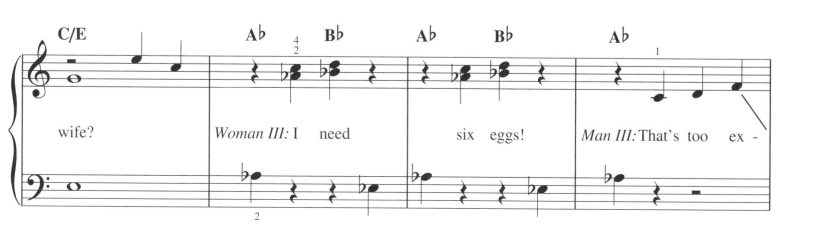

wife? | *Woman III:* I need six eggs! | *Man III:* That's too ex-

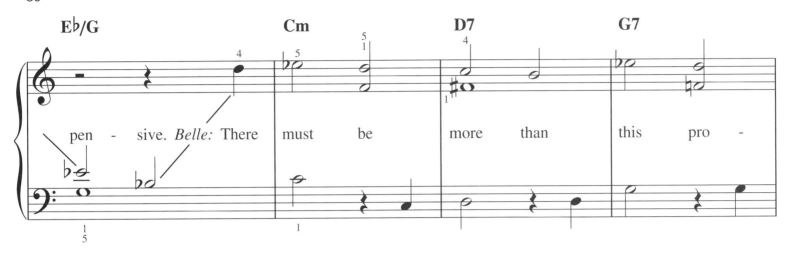

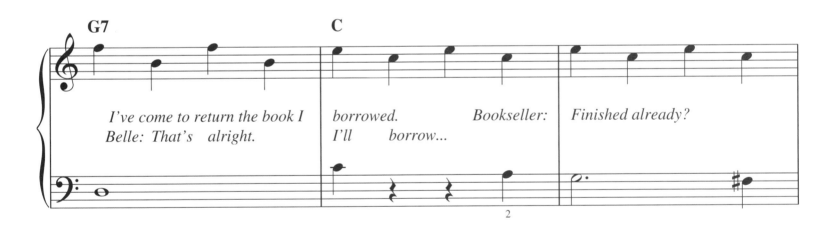

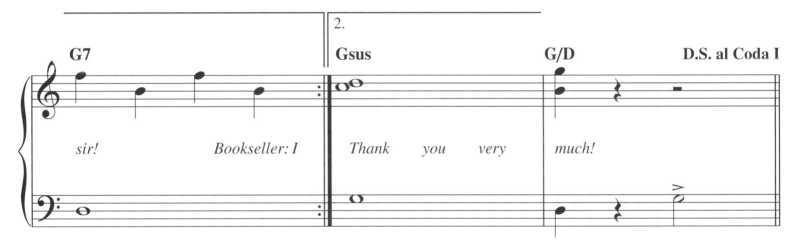

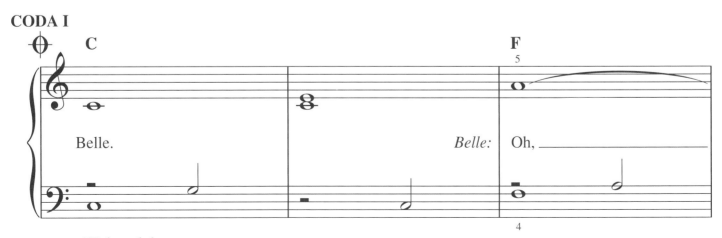

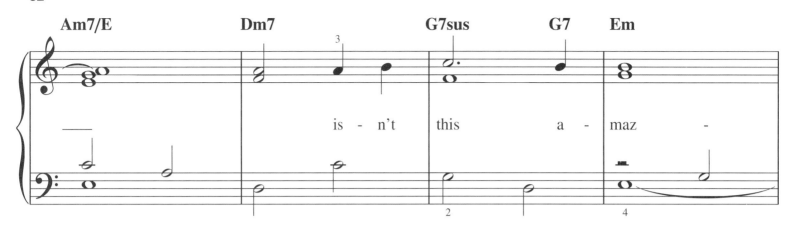

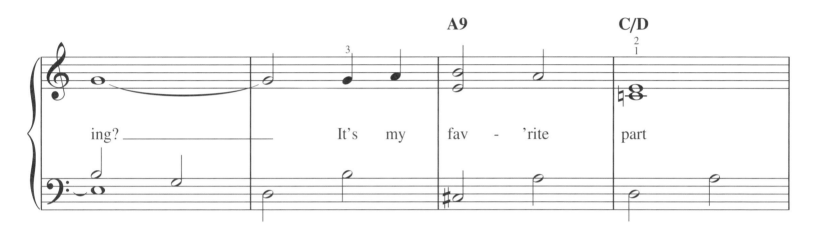

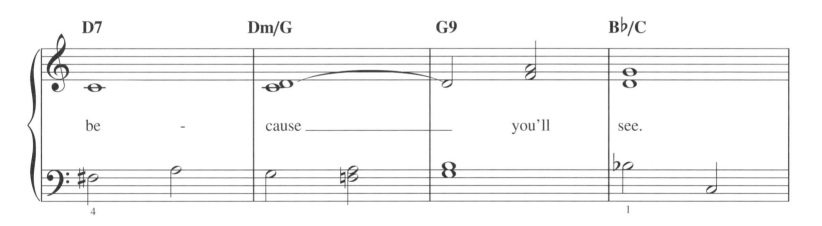

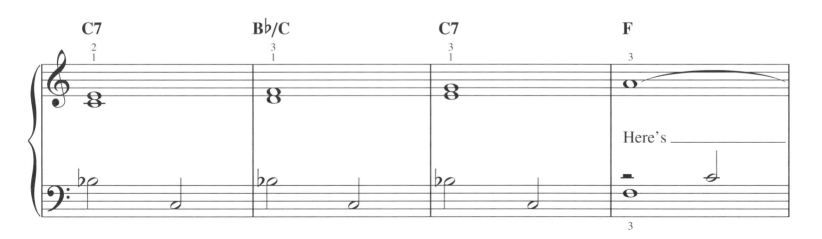

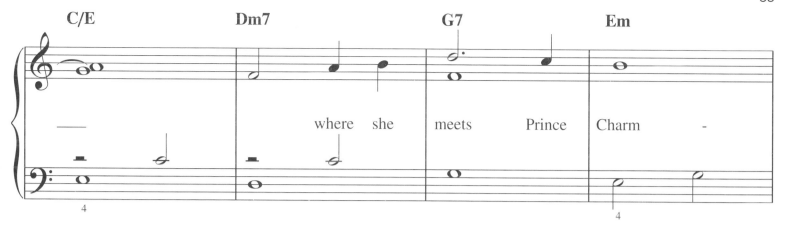

where she meets Prince Charm -

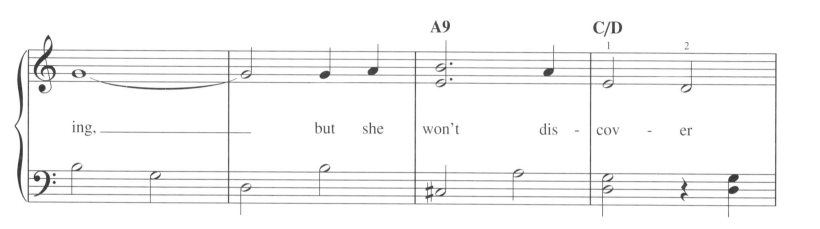

ing, _____ but she won't dis - cov - er

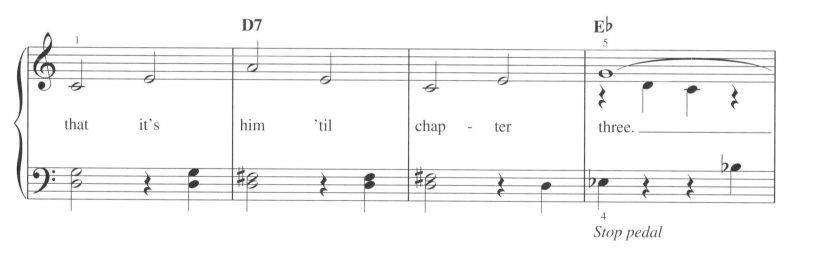

that it's him 'til chap - ter three. _____

Stop pedal

Woman: Now, it's no
Townsfolk: Look there she

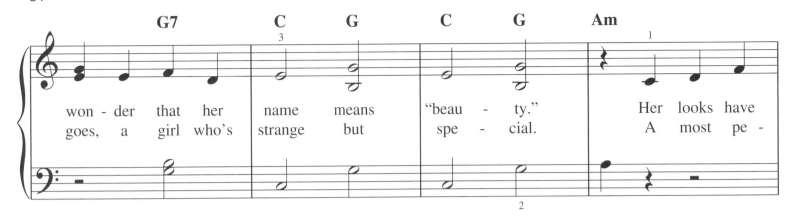

won - der that her name means "beau - ty." Her looks have
goes, a girl who's strange but spe - cial. A most pe -

got no par - al - lel.
cu - liar mad -'moi - selle.

Shopkeeper: But be - hind that fair fa -
It's a pit - y and a

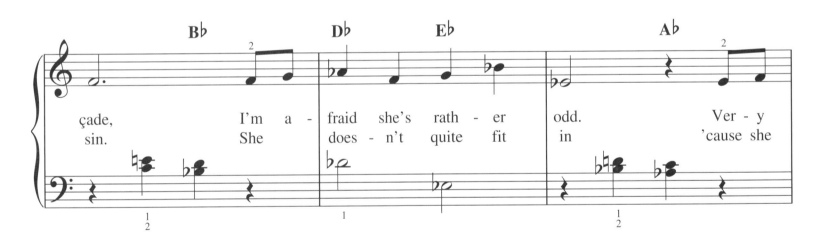

çade, I'm a - fraid she's rath - er odd. Ver - y
sin. She does - n't quite fit in 'cause she

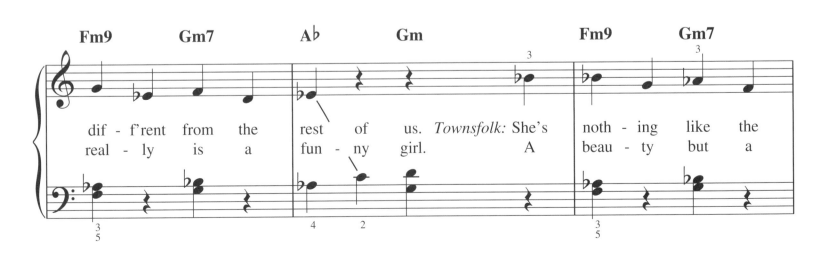

dif - f'rent from the rest of us. *Townsfolk:* She's noth - ing like the
real - ly is a fun - ny girl. A beau - ty but a

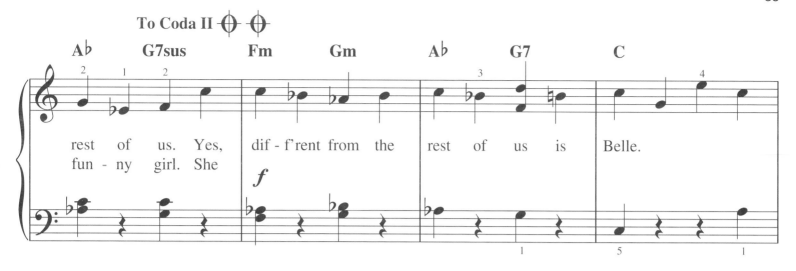

rest of us. Yes,
fun - ny girl. She

dif - f'rent from the rest of us is Belle.

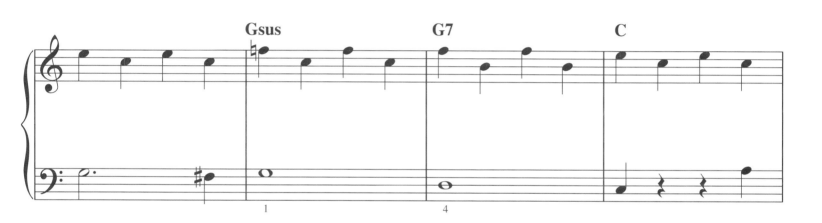

Pompously

Gaston: Right from the

mo - ment when I met her, saw her, I said she's

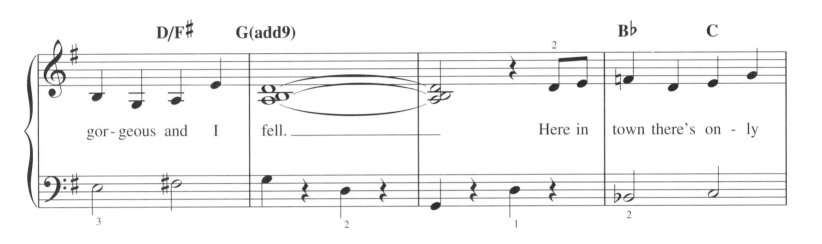

gor - geous and I fell. _____ Here in town there's on - ly

she who is beau - ti - ful as me, so I'm mak - ing plans to

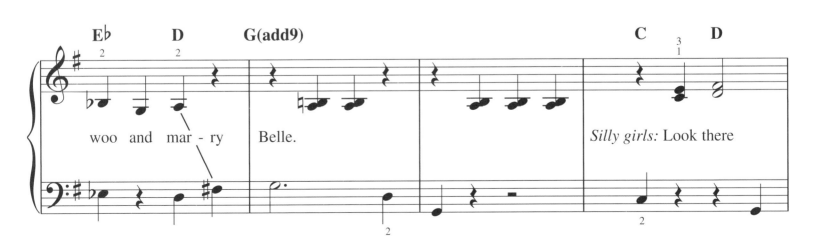

woo and mar - ry Belle. *Silly girls:* Look there

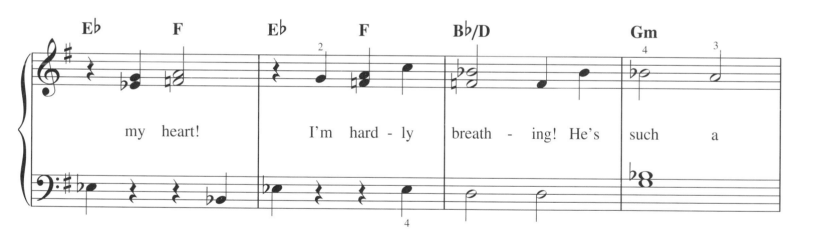

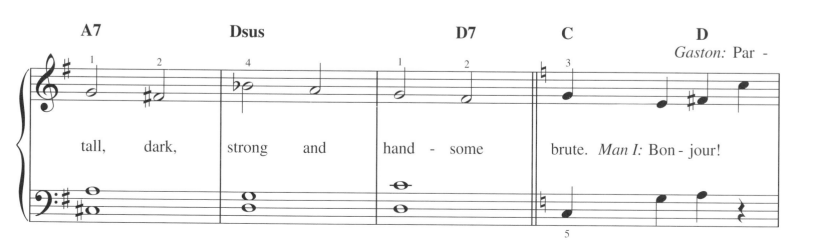

38

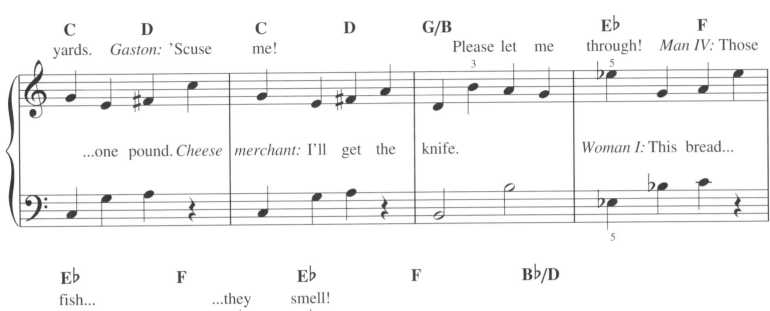

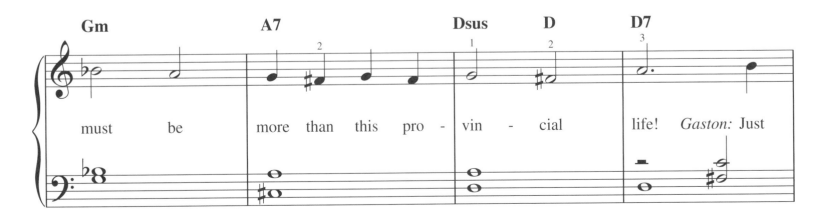

D.S.S. al Coda II

watch   I'm   go - ing   to   make   Belle   my   wife!

CODA II

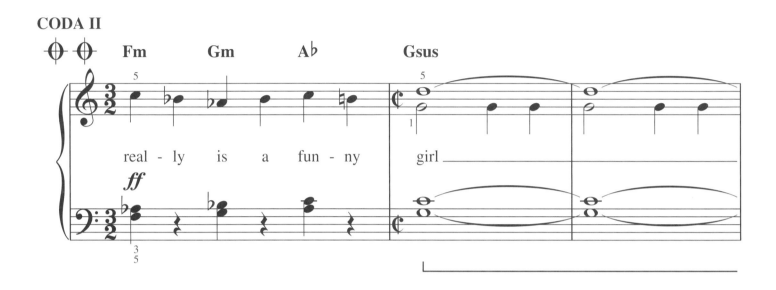

real - ly   is   a   fun - ny   girl

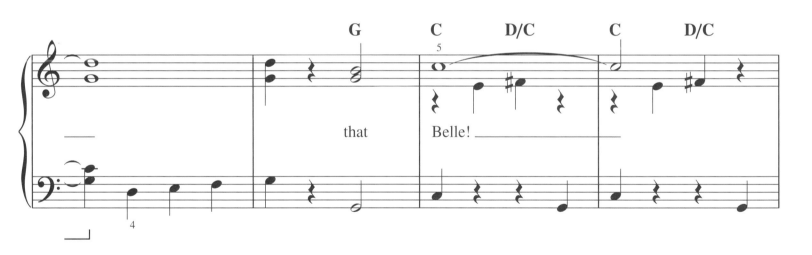

that   Belle!

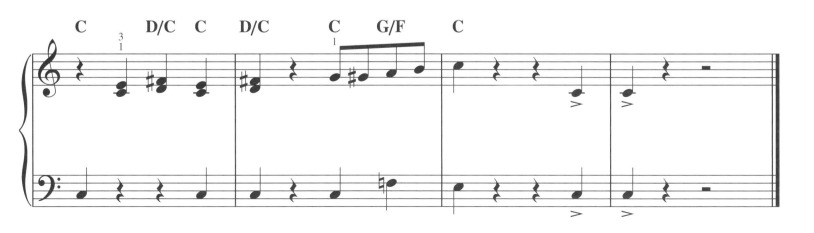

CAN YOU FEEL THE LOVE TONIGHT

from Walt Disney Pictures' THE LION KING

Music by ELTON JOHN
Lyrics by TIM RICE

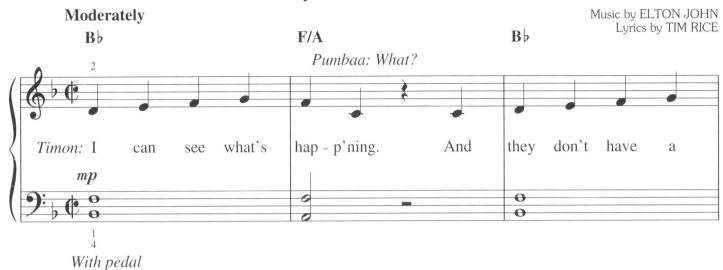

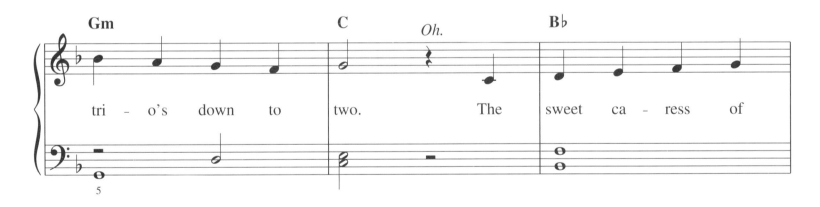

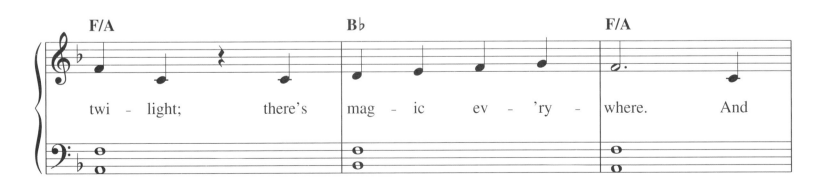

41

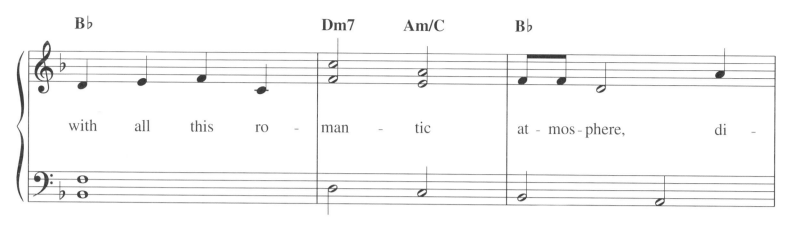

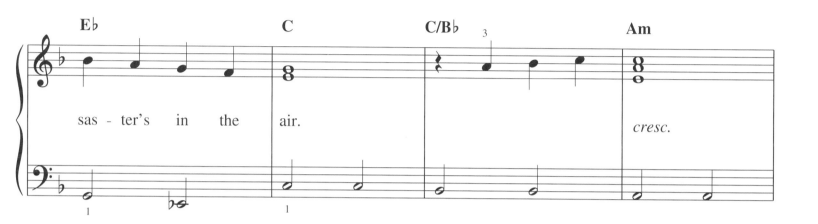

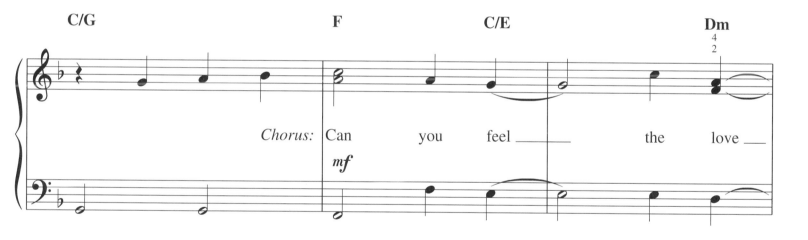

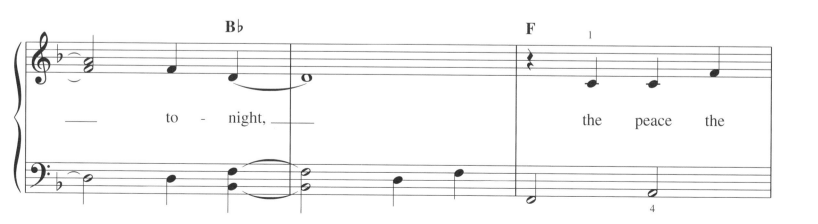

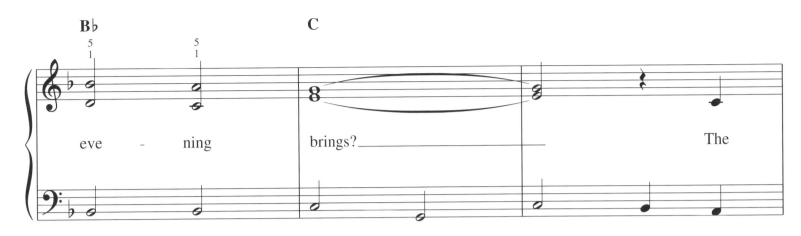

eve - ning   brings? _____   The

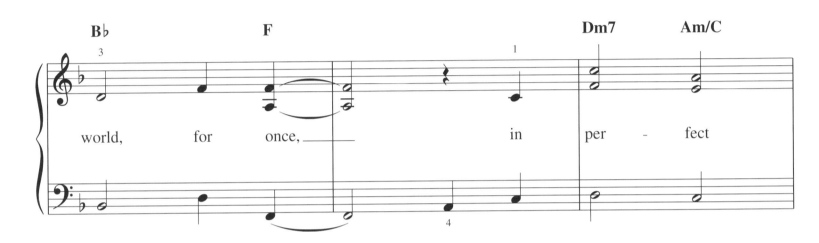

world,   for   once, _____   in   per - fect

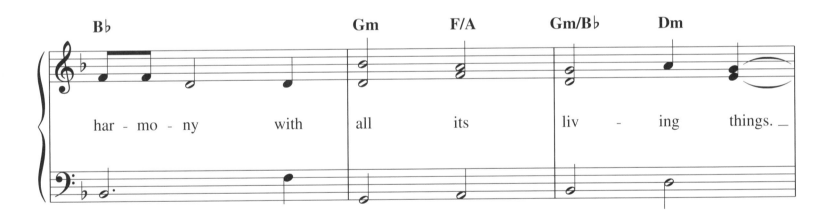

har - mo - ny   with   all   its   liv - ing   things. _

dim.   *Simba:* So   man - y   things   to

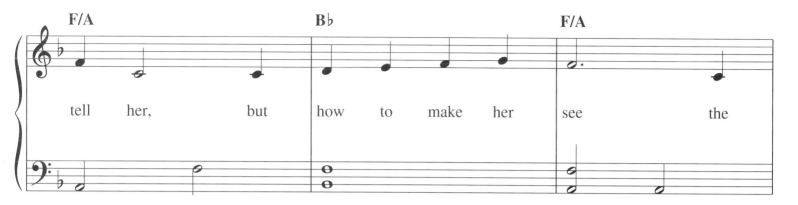

tell her, but how to make her see the

truth a - bout my past? Im - pos - si - ble. She'd turn a - way from

me. _____ *Nala:* He's hold - ing back, he's hid - ing. But

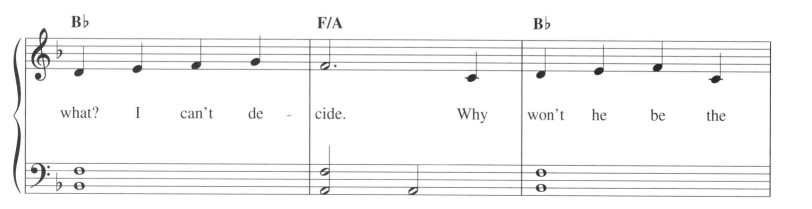

what? I can't de - cide. Why won't he be the

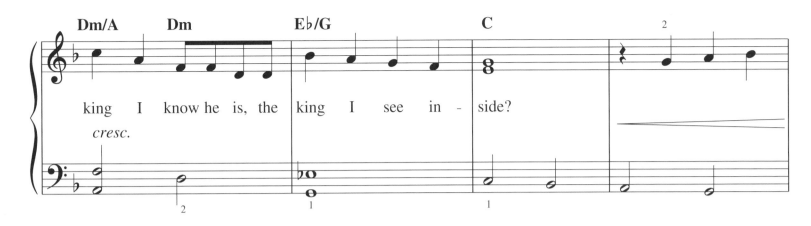

king I know he is, the king I see in - side?

cresc.

Chorus:
Can you feel ____ the love ____ to - night, ____

mf

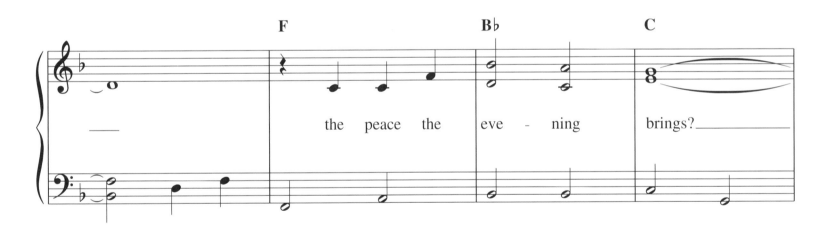

____ the peace the eve - ning brings? ____

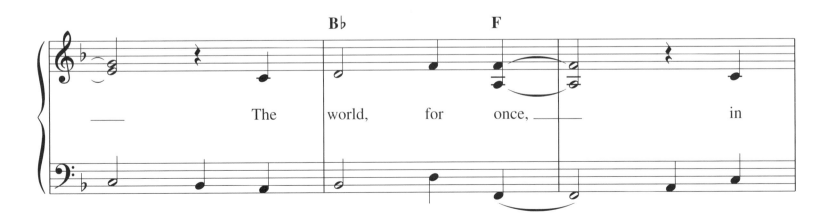

____ The world, for once, ____ in

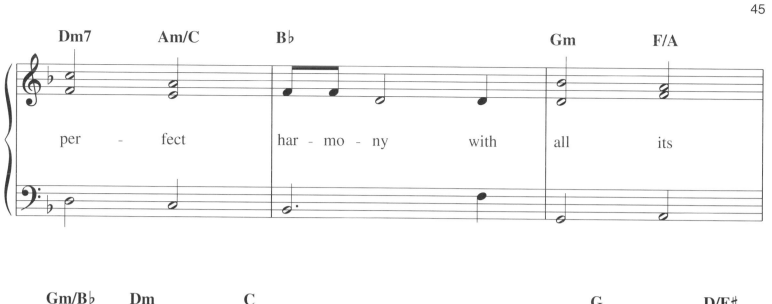

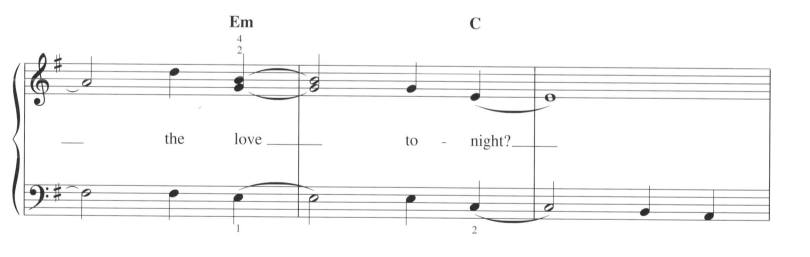

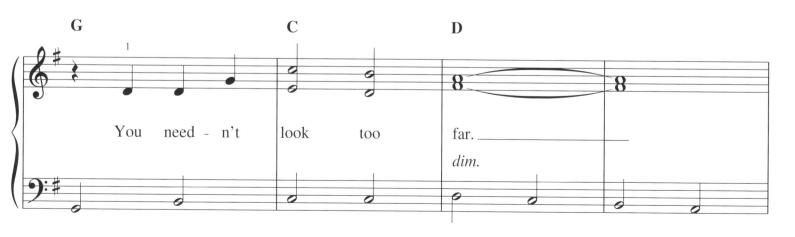

46

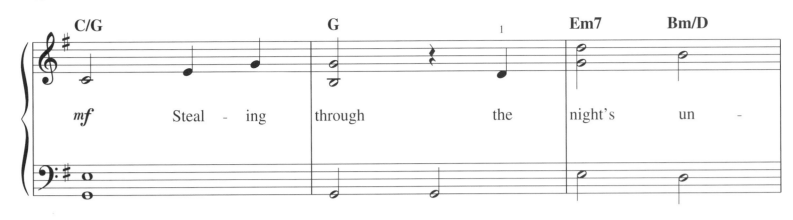

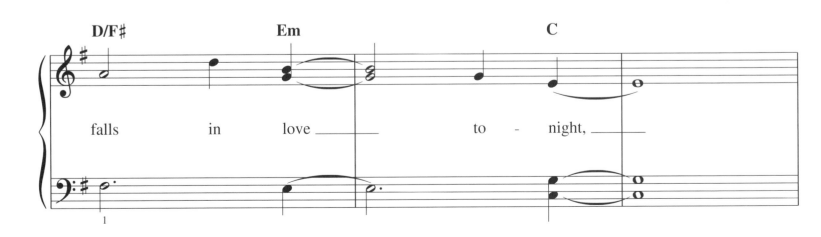

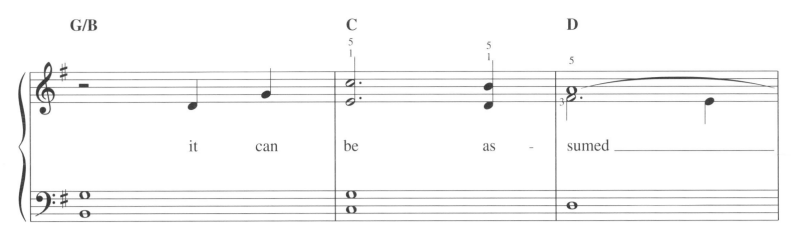

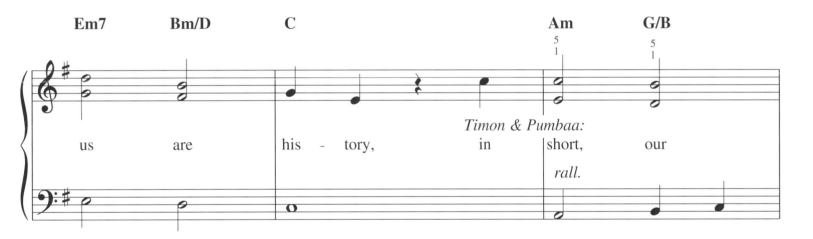

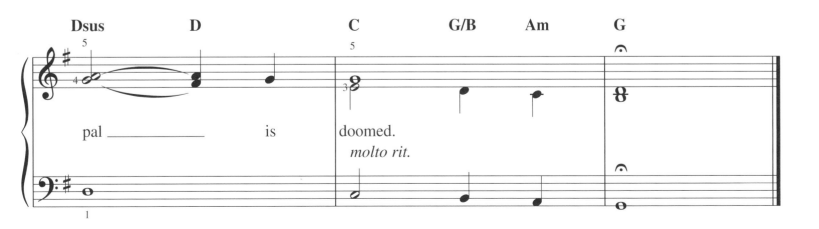

COLORS OF THE WIND

from Walt Disney's POCAHONTAS

Music by ALAN MENKEN
Lyrics by STEPHEN SCHWARTZ

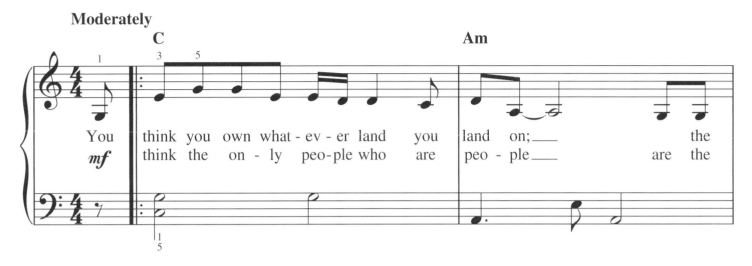

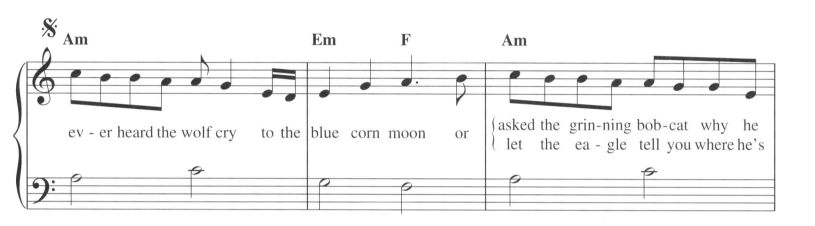

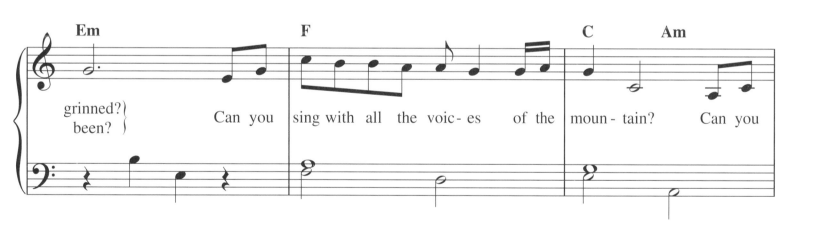

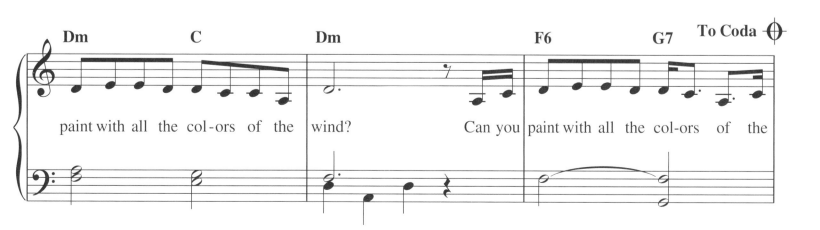

C   **Dm7**   **G7**   **C**

wind?_____ Come run the hid - den pine trails of the
rain-storm and the riv - er are my

Am   **C**

for - est,_____ come taste the sun - sweet ber - ries of the
broth - ers:_____ the her - on and the ot - ter are my

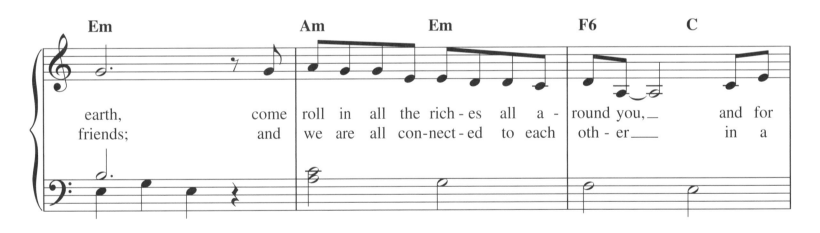

Em   **Am**   **Em**   **F6**   **C**

earth, come roll in all the rich - es all a - round you,_____ and for
friends; and we are all con-nect-ed to each oth - er_____ in a

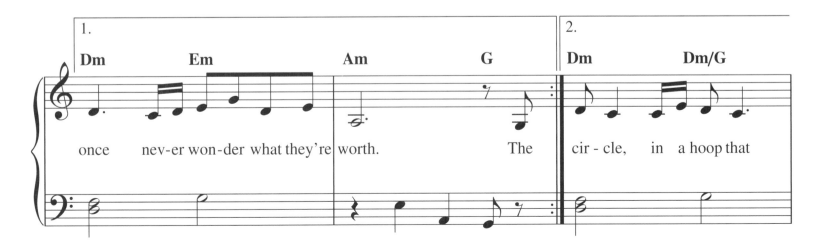

1.
Dm   **Em**   **Am**   **G**

once nev-er won-der what they're worth. The

2.
Dm   **Dm/G**

cir - cle, in a hoop that

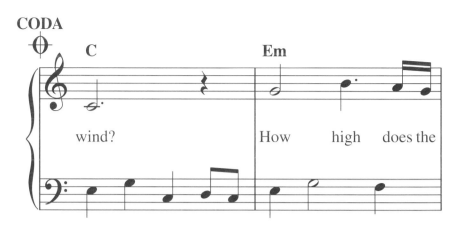

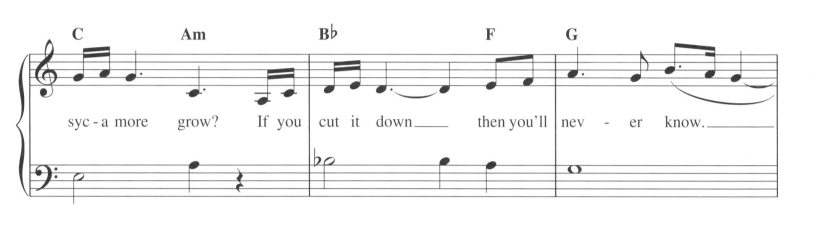

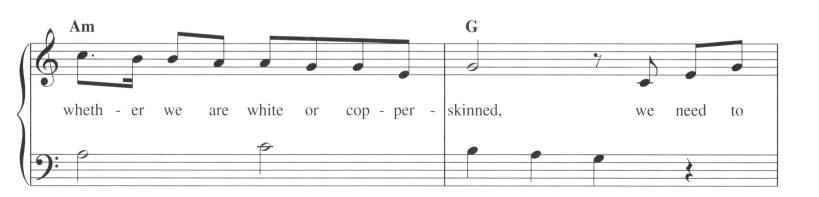

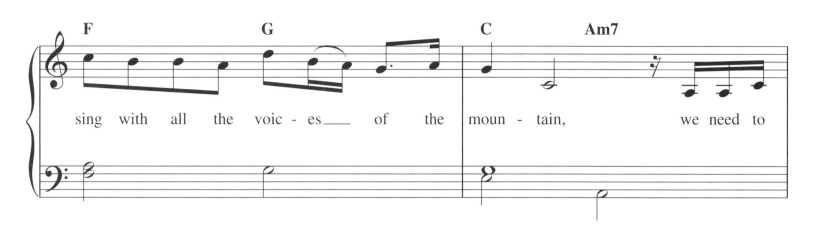

sing with all the voic - es___ of the moun - tain, we need to

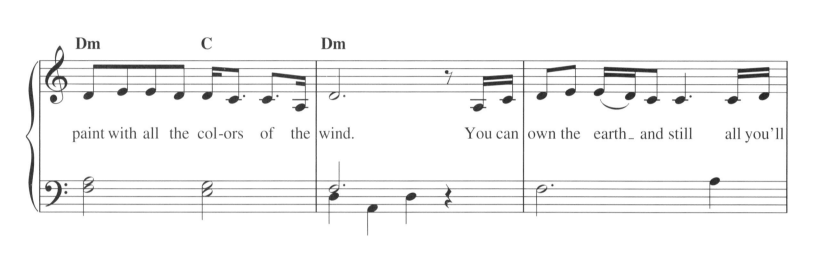

paint with all the col-ors of the wind. You can own the earth_ and still all you'll

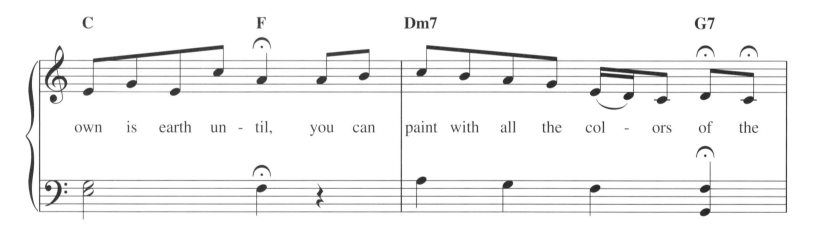

own is earth un - til, you can paint with all the col - ors of the

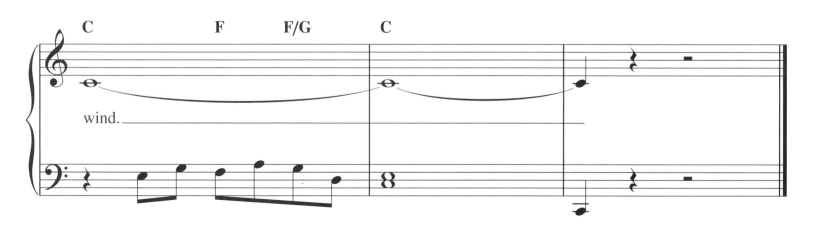

wind.___

HAKUNA MATATA
from Walt Disney Pictures' THE LION KING

Music by ELTON JOHN
Lyrics by TIM RICE

Freely

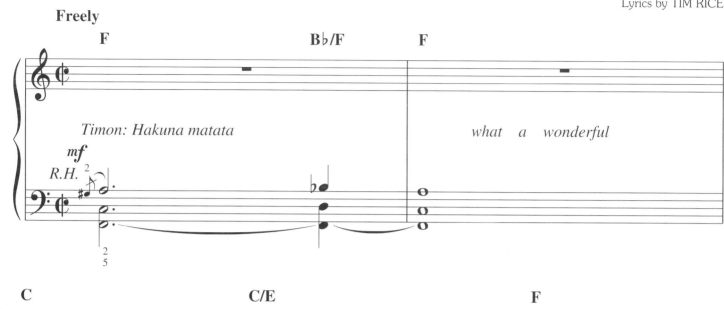

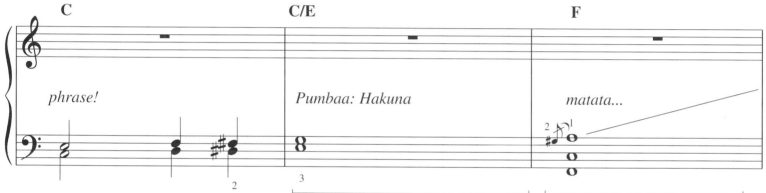

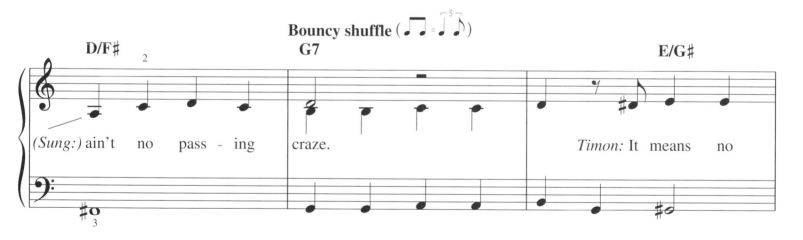

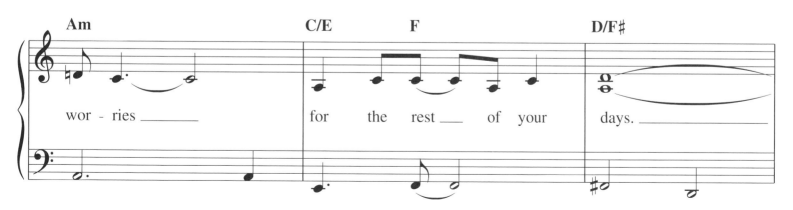

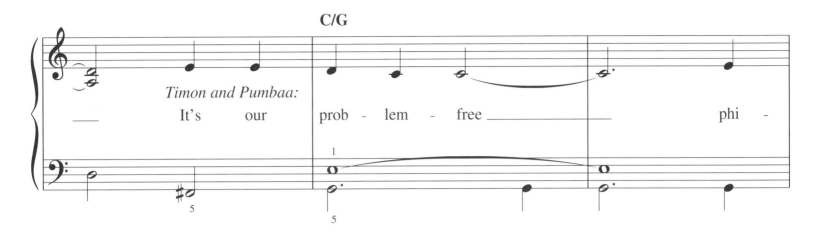

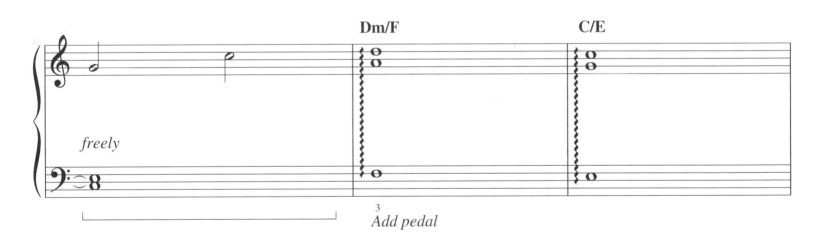

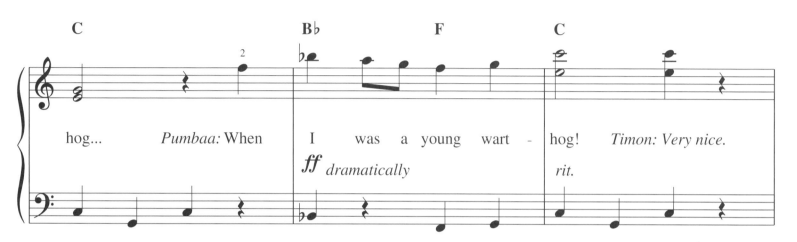

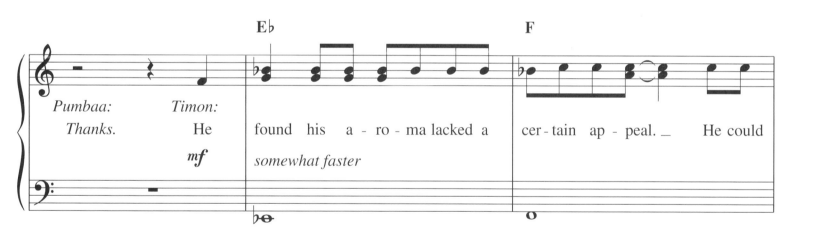

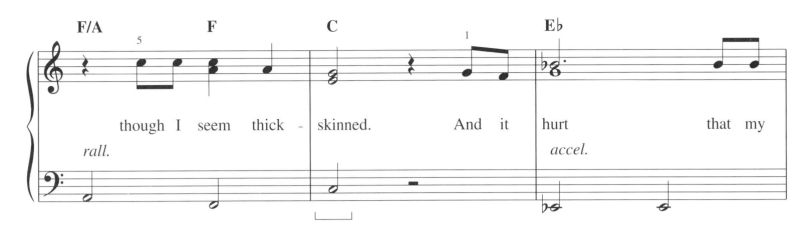

though I seem thick - skinned. And it hurt that my
rall. *accel.*

friends nev - er stood down - wind!
(Spoken:) And, oh, ___ the
rit.

Timon:
shame! He was a -
a tempo

Pumbaa:
shamed! Thought of chang - in' my

Timon:
name! Oh, what's in a

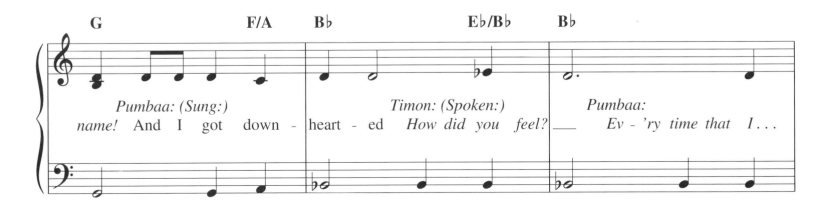

Pumbaa: (Sung:)
name! And I got down - heart - ed *How did you feel?* ___

Timon: (Spoken:)

Pumbaa:
Ev - 'ry time that I . . .

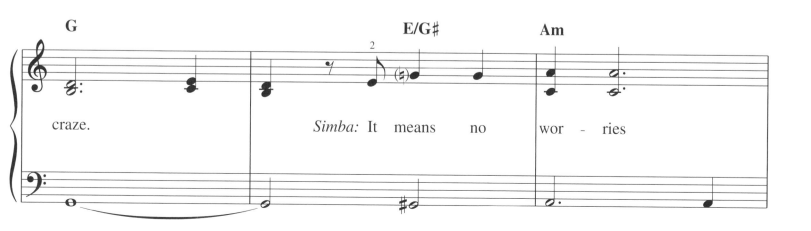

for the rest ___ of your days. ___
Timon: Yeah, sing it kid!
Timon and Simba: It's our

prob - lem - free ___
Pumbaa: phi - los - o - phy. ___

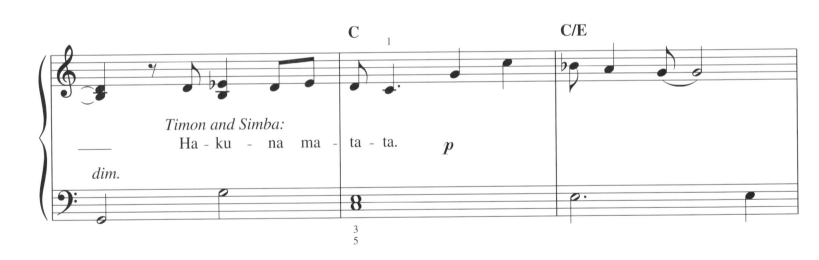

Timon and Simba:
Ha - ku - na ma - ta - ta. *p*
dim.

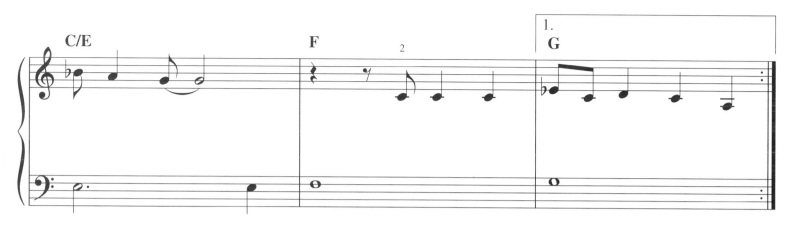

All: (Spoken:)   *Hakuna   matata.*   *Hakuna   matata.*

cresc. poco a poco

Add pedal

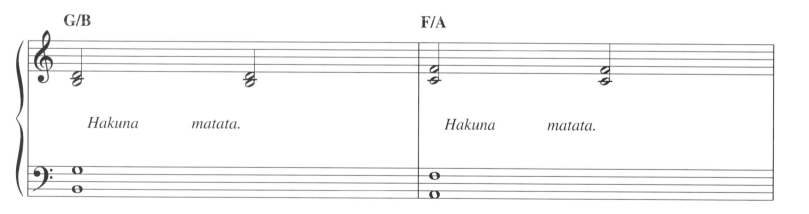

Hakuna   matata.   *Hakuna   matata.*

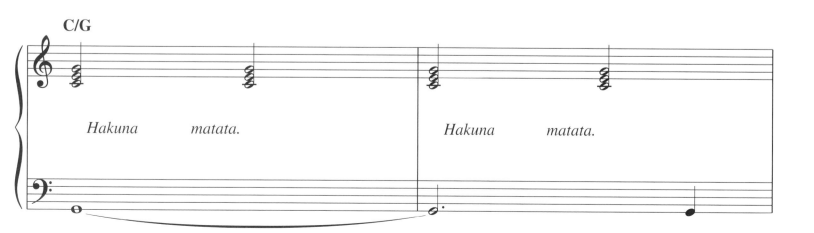

Hakuna   matata.   *Hakuna   matata.*

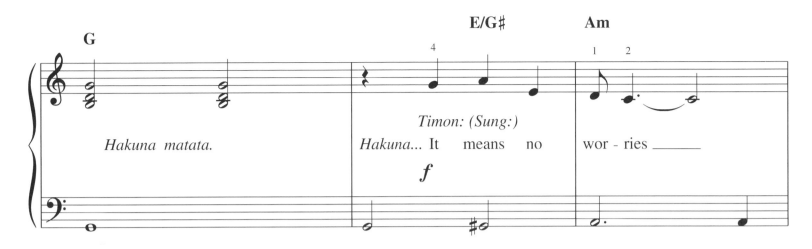

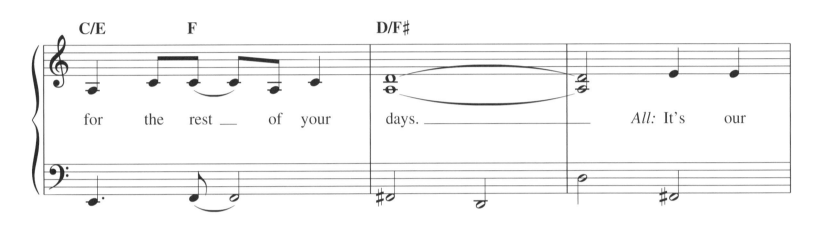

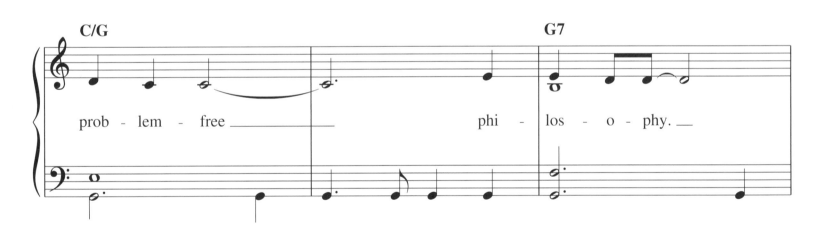

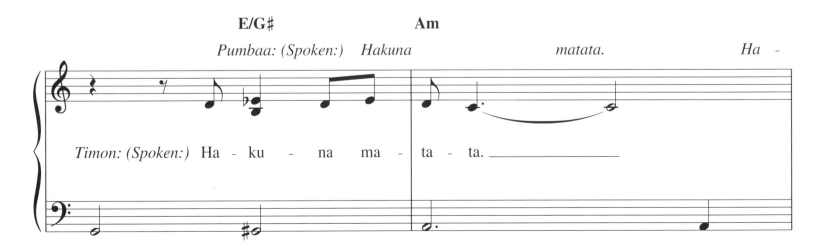

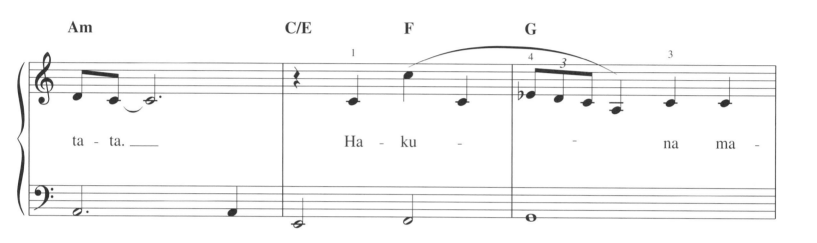

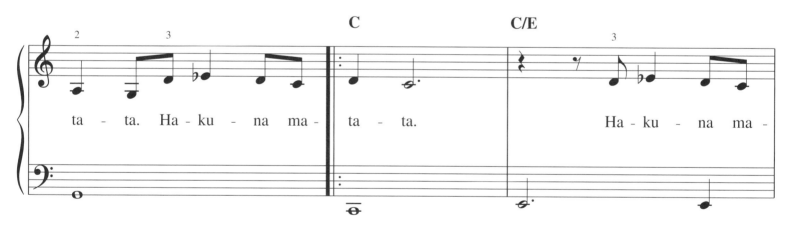

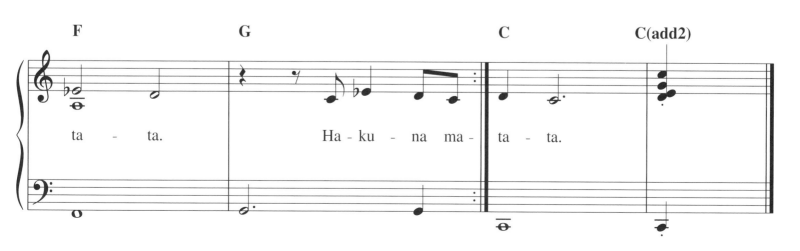

FRIEND LIKE ME
from Walt Disney's ALADDIN

Lyrics by HOWARD ASHMAN
Music by ALAN MENKEN

Moderately bright

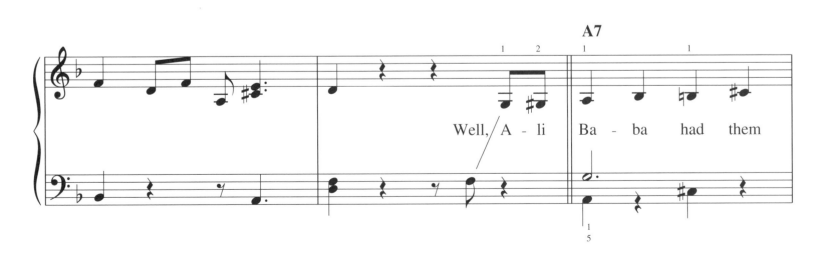

Well, A - li Ba - ba had them

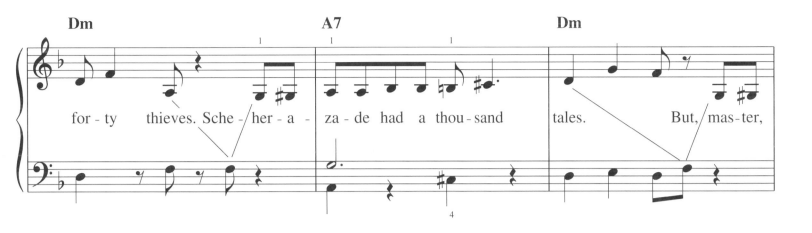

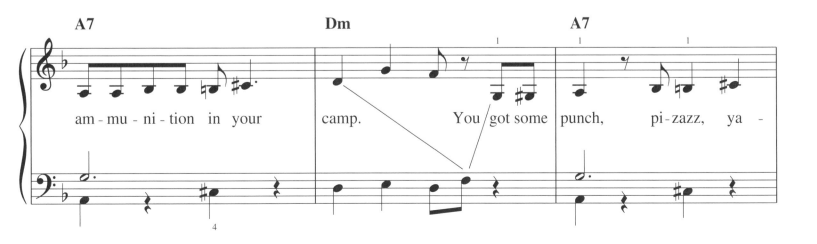

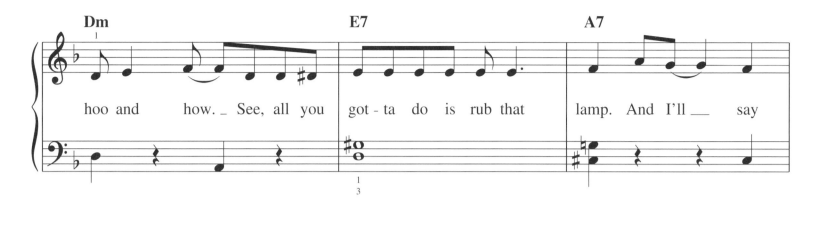

hoo and how._ See, all you | got-ta do is rub that | lamp. And I'll ___ say

Mis - ter A - | lad-din sir, ___ what | will your plea-sure

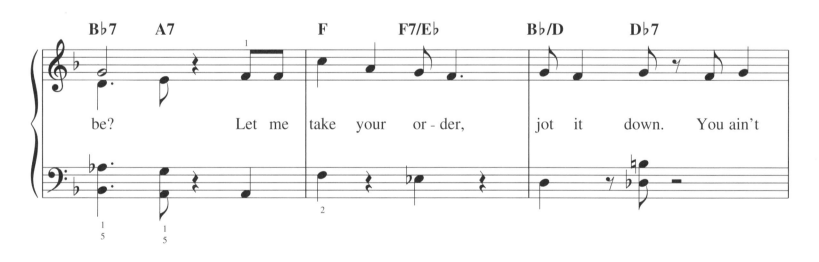

be? Let me | take your or-der, | jot it down. You ain't

nev - er had a friend like | me. No no no. | Life is your

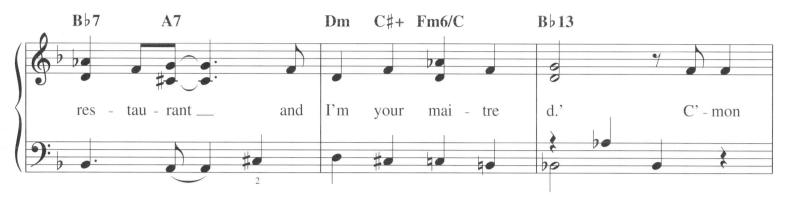

res - tau - rant ___ and I'm your mai - tre d.' C'- mon

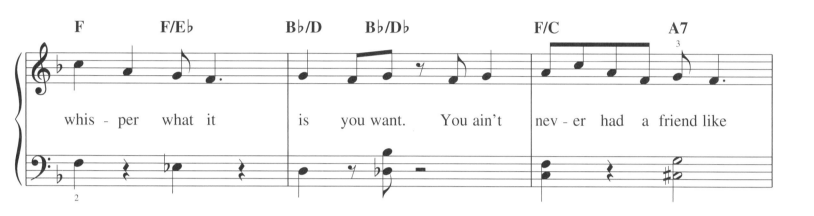

whis - per what it is you want. You ain't nev - er had a friend like

me. Yes, sir, we pride our - selves on ser - vice. You're the

boss, the king, the shah. Say what you wish. ___ It's

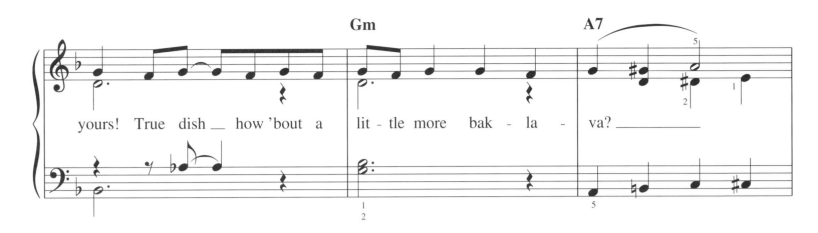

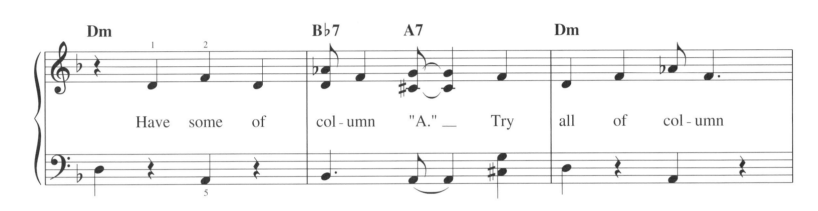

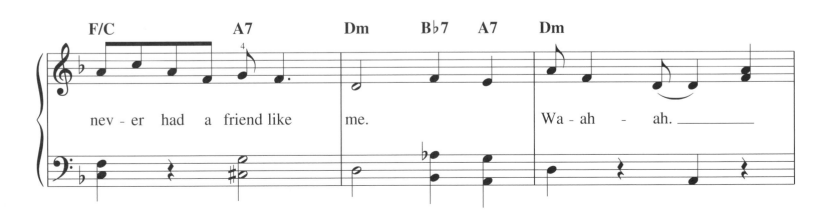

Oh my.   Wa - ah - ah. ___   No   no.

Wa - ah - ah. _____   Na   na   na. __

Can your friends do   this?   Can your friends do

that?   Can your friends pull   this

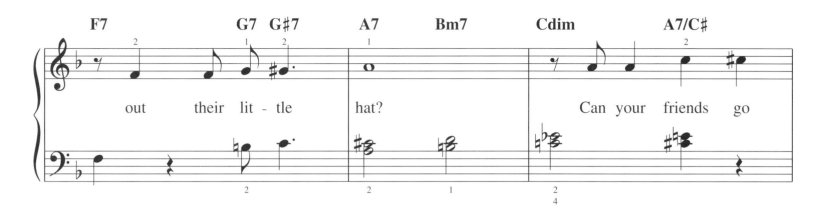

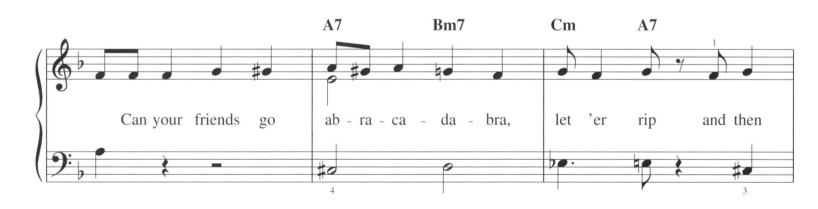

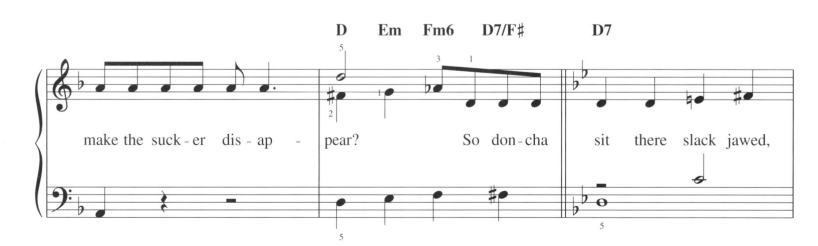

buggy eyed. I'm here to answer all your mid-day prayers. You got me

bona-fi-de cer-ti-fied. __ You got a ge-nie for your chargé d'af-

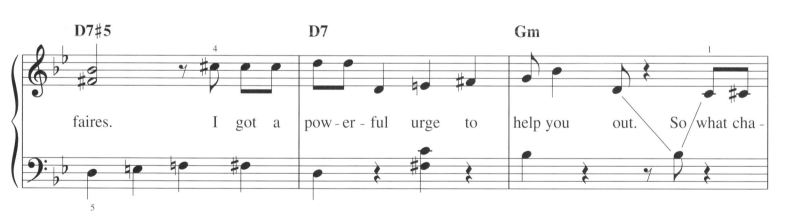

faires. I got a pow-er-ful urge to help you out. So what cha-

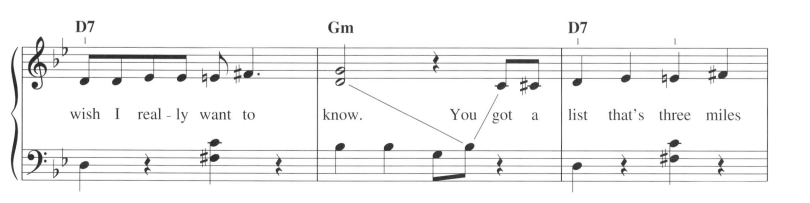

wish I real-ly want to know. You got a list that's three miles

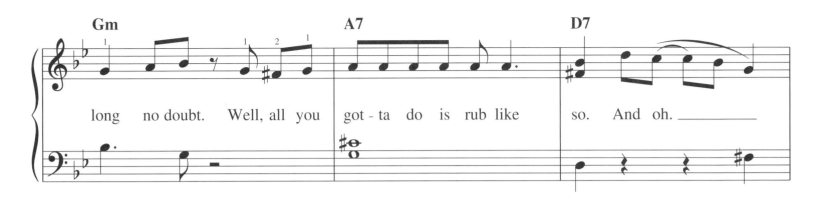

long no doubt. Well, all you gotta do is rub like so. And oh._____

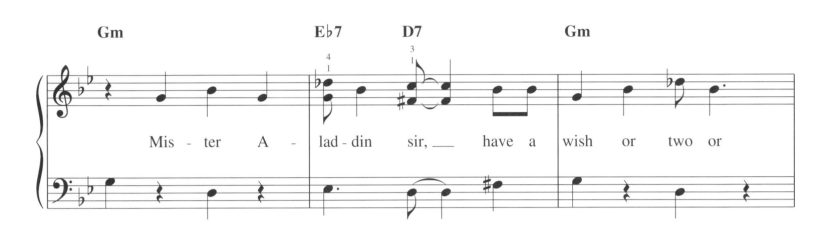

Mis - ter A - lad - din sir,___ have a wish or two or

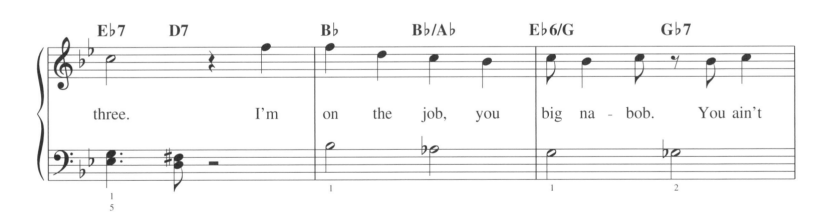

three. I'm on the job, you big na - bob. You ain't

nev - er had a friend, nev - er had a friend, you ain't nev - er had a friend, nev - er

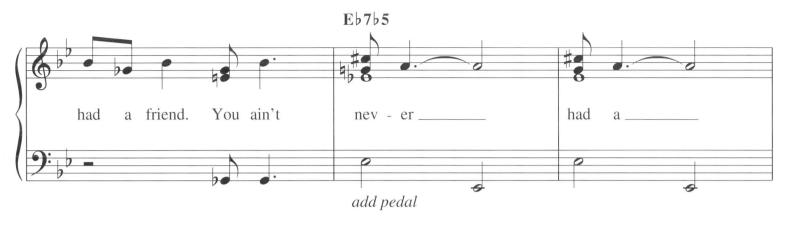

Eb7b5

had a friend. You ain't nev - er _____ had a _____

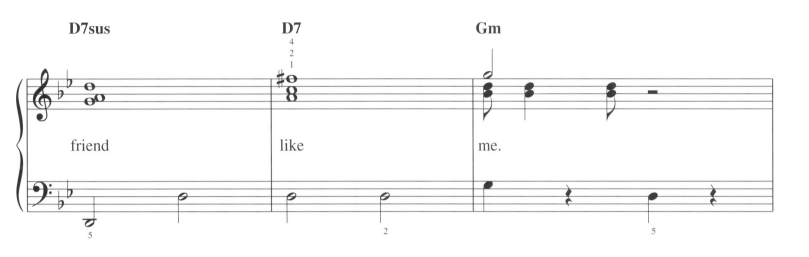

D7sus   D7   Gm

friend   like   me.

add pedal

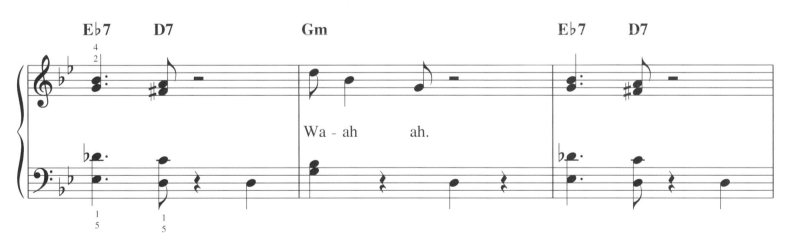

Eb7   D7   Gm   Eb7   D7

Wa - ah   ah.

Gm   Eb7   D7   Eb7   D7   Gm

Wa ah   ah.   You ain't nev-er had a friend like   me. Ha!

GO THE DISTANCE

from Walt Disney Pictures' HERCULES

Music by ALAN MENKEN
Lyrics by DAVID ZIPPEL

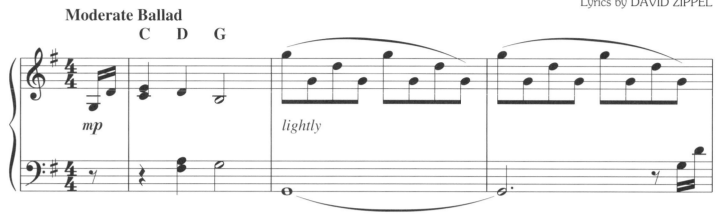

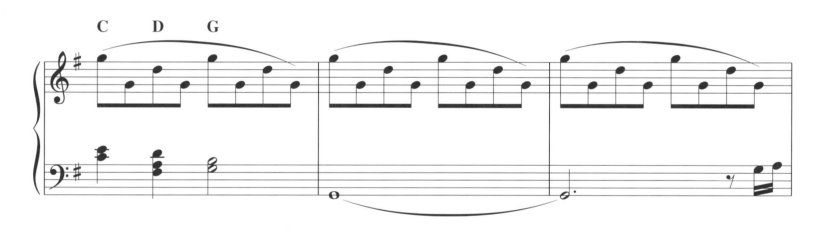

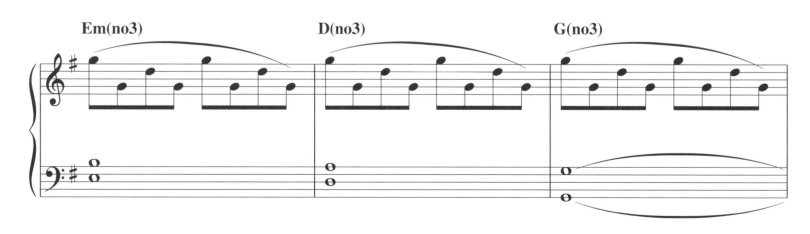

I have of - ten dreamed of a far - off place where a

great warm wel-come will be wait - ing for me. Where the crowds will cheer when they

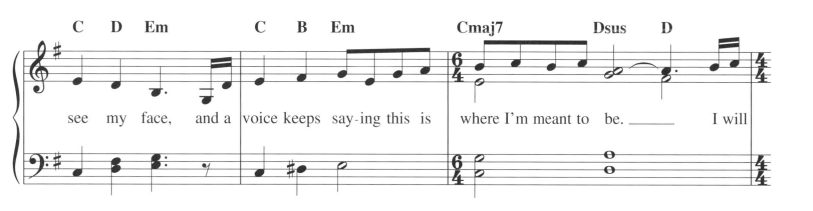

see my face, and a voice keeps say-ing this is where I'm meant to be. _____ I will

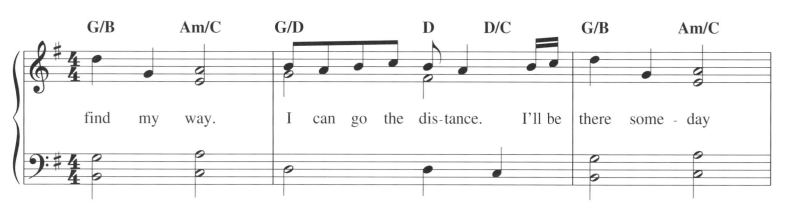

find my way. I can go the dis-tance. I'll be there some - day

if I can be strong. I know ev - 'ry mile will be worth my

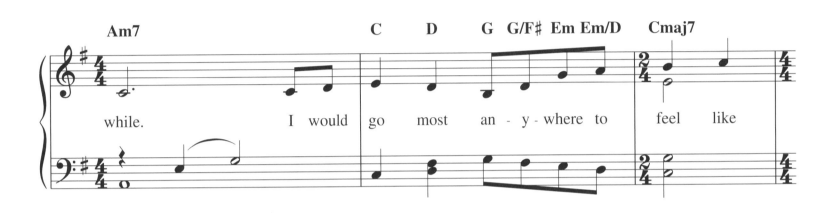

while. I would go most an - y - where to feel like

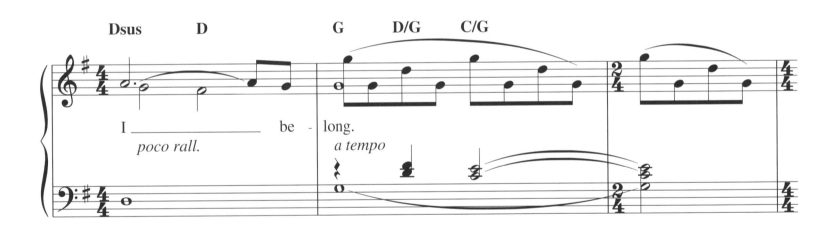

I _____ be - long.

poco rall. *a tempo*

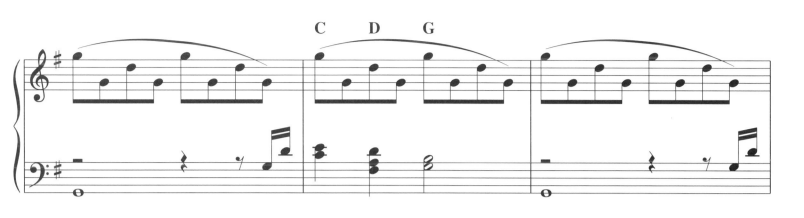

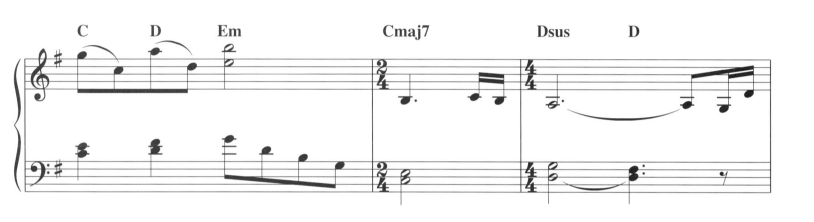

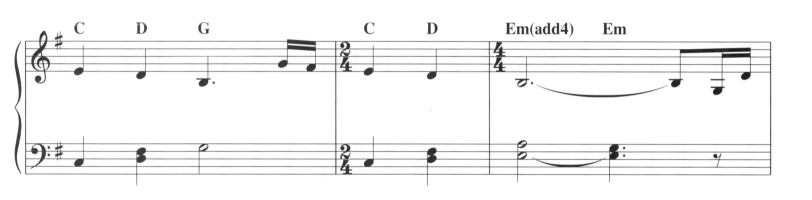

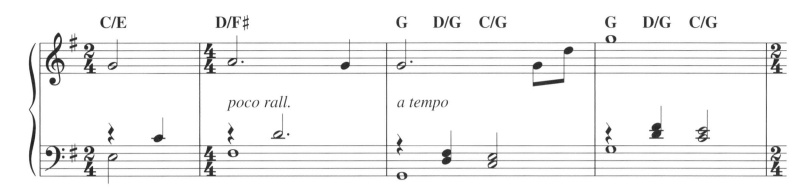

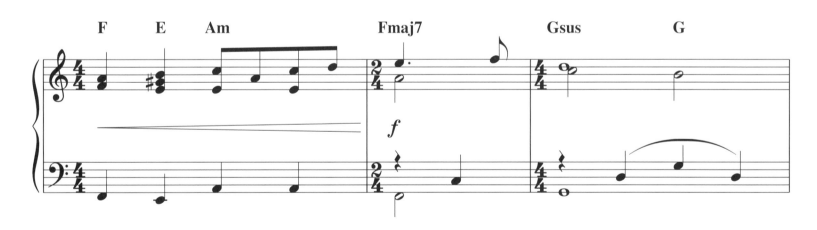

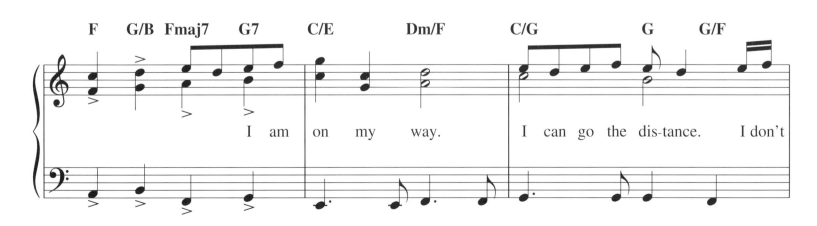

I am on my way. I can go the dis-tance. I don't

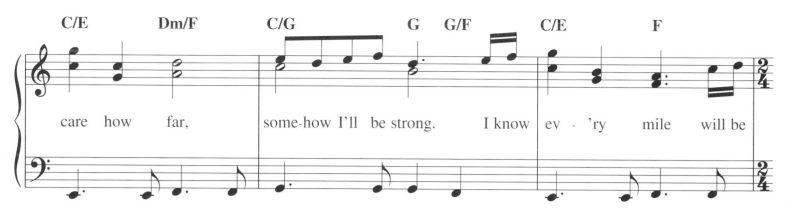

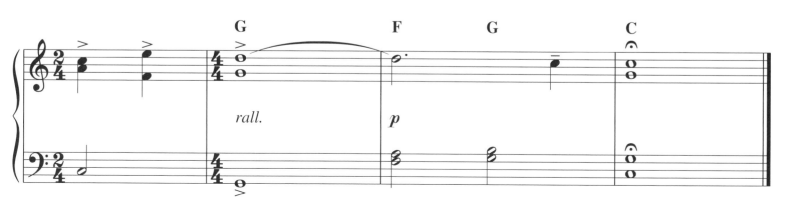

GOD HELP THE OUTCASTS

from Walt Disney's THE HUNCHBACK OF NOTRE DAME

Music by ALAN MENKEN
Lyrics by STEPHEN SCHWARTZ

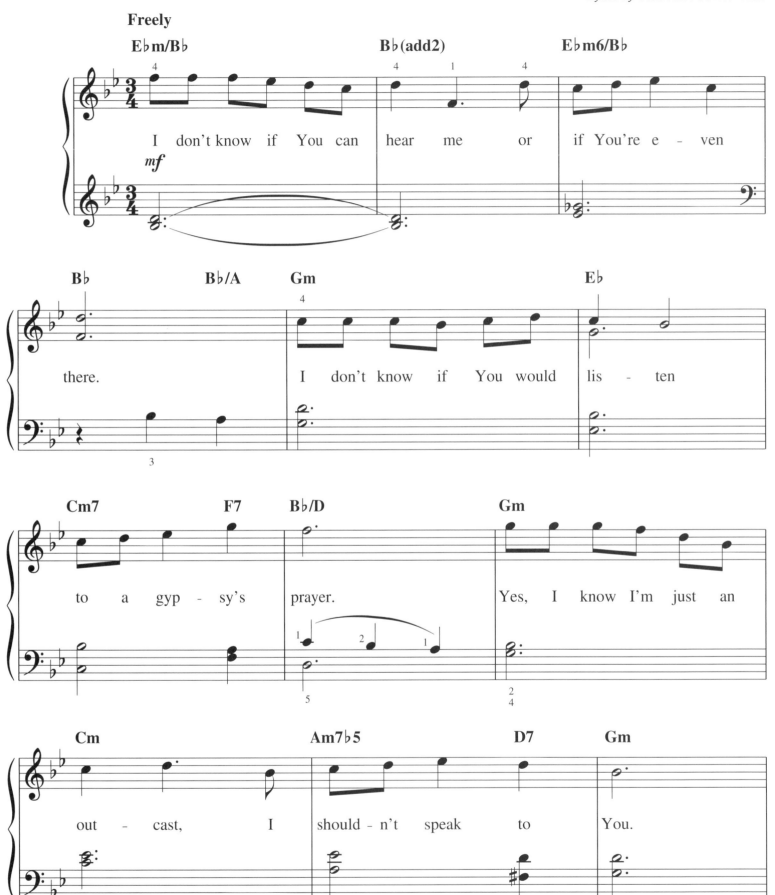

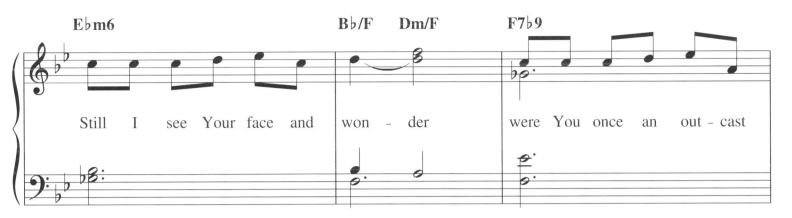

E♭m6 · **B♭/F** · **Dm/F** · **F7♭9**

Still I see Your face and won - der | won - der | were You once an out - cast

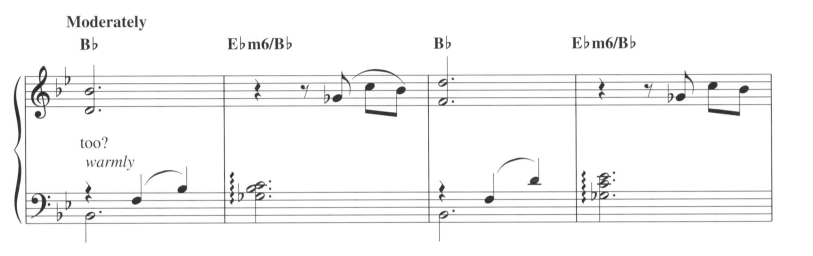

Moderately

B♭ · **E♭m6/B♭** · **B♭** · **E♭m6/B♭**

too?
warmly

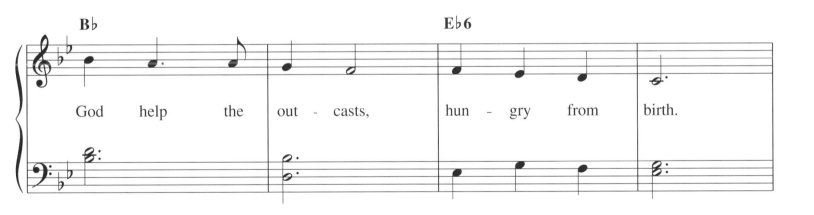

B♭ · **E♭6**

God help the out - casts, hun - gry from birth.

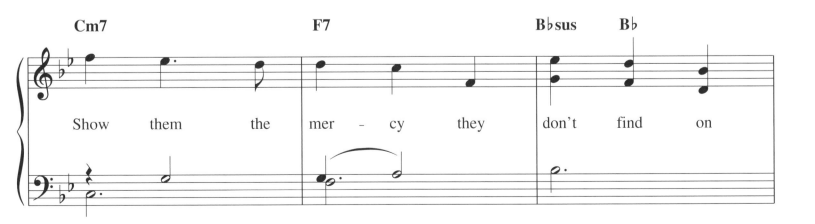

Cm7 · **F7** · **B♭sus** · **B♭**

Show them the mer - cy they don't find on

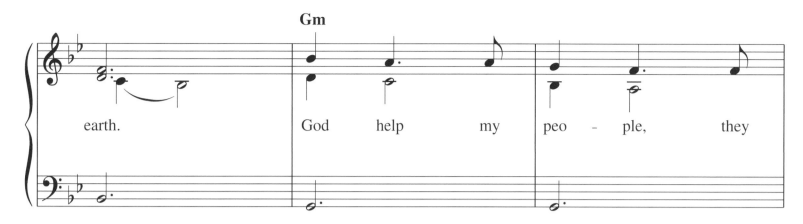

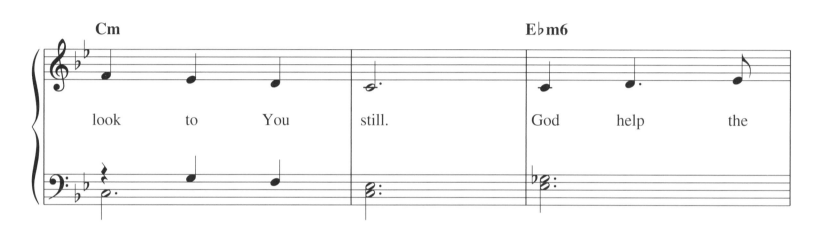

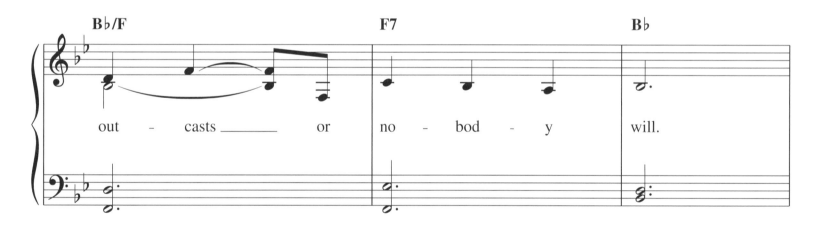

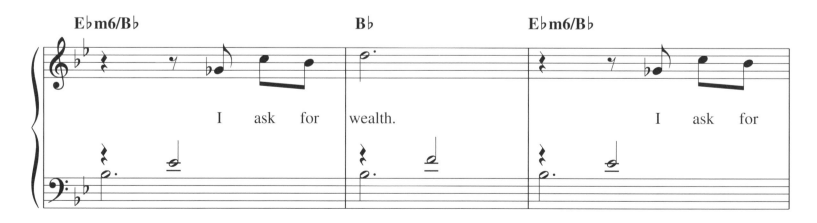

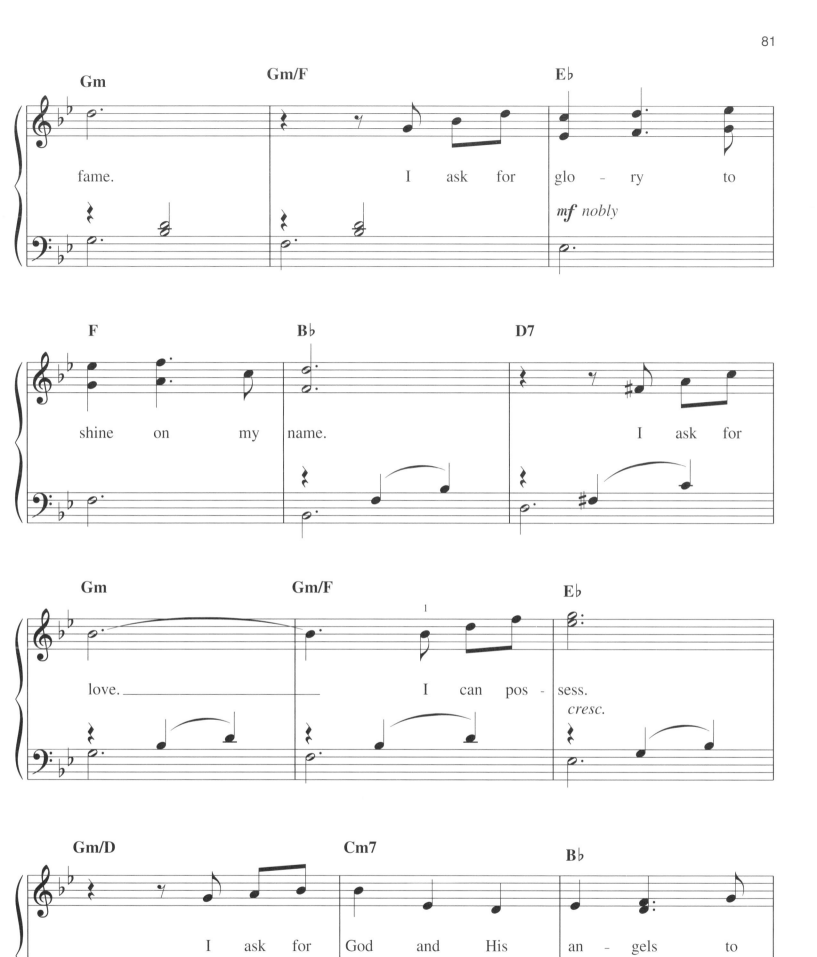

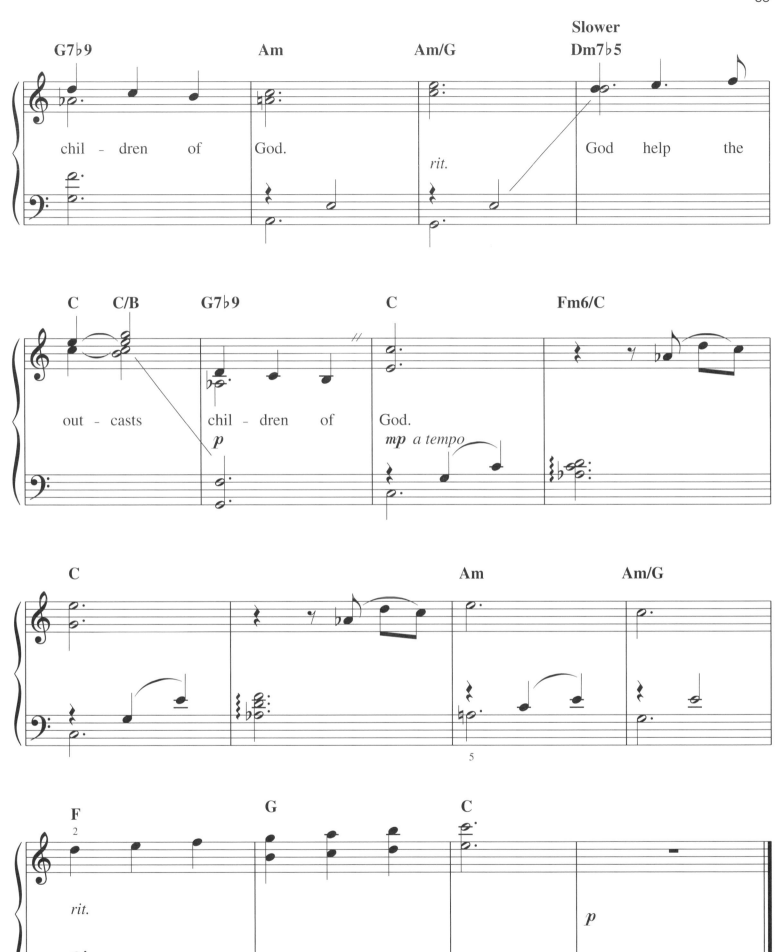

HAWAIIAN ROLLER COASTER RIDE

from Walt Disney's LILO & STITCH

Words and Music by ALAN SILVESTRI
and MARK KEALI'I HO'OMALU

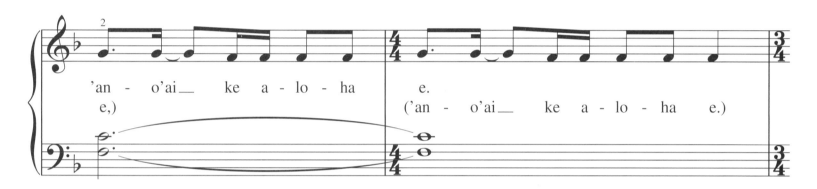

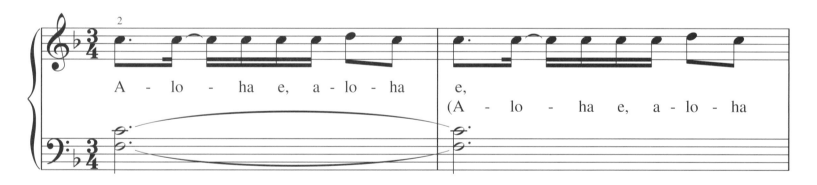

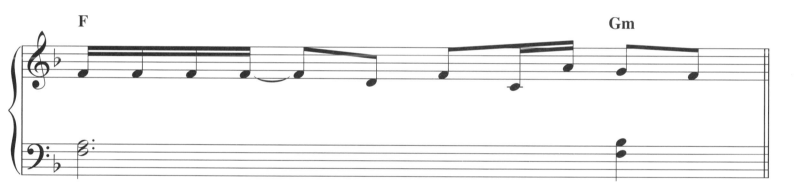

Lead:
1.,3. There's no___ place I'd rath - er be   than on my surf - board out at sea.

All:
2. There's no___ place I'd rath - er be   than on the sea - shore dry, wet, free.

Chorus:

Chorus:

Children's chorus

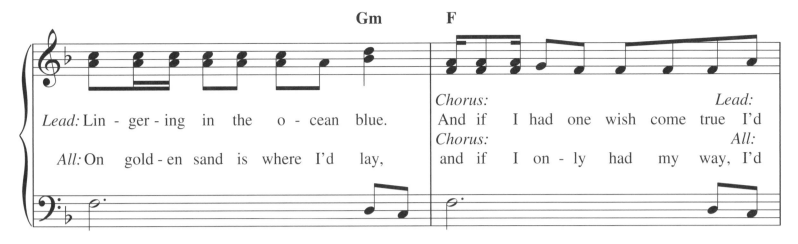

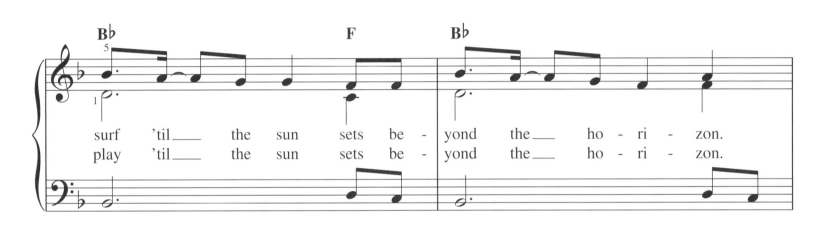

F   **Gm**   **F**

ride.
ride.

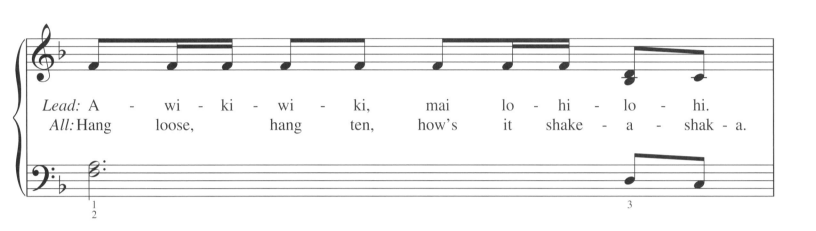

Lead: A - wi - ki - wi - ki, mai lo - hi - lo - hi.
All: Hang loose, hang ten, how's it shake - a - shak - a.

Bb6

Chorus: La - we mai i ko pa - pa he - 'e na - lu.
No wor - ry, no fear. Ain't____ no big - gy, brah - da.

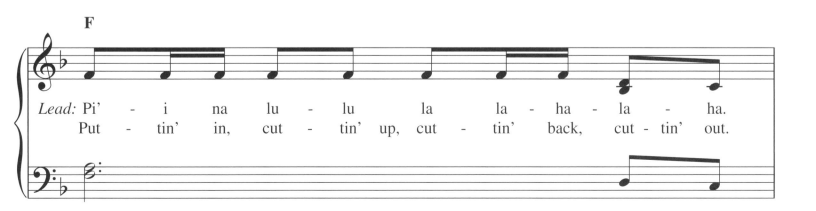

F

Lead: Pi' - i na lu - lu la la - ha - la - ha.
Put - tin' in, cut - tin' up, cut - tin' back, cut - tin' out.

Bb6   **To Coda**

Chorus: O   ka   mo - a - na   ha - nu - pa - nu - pa.
Front   side,   back   side,   goof - y   foot - ed   wipe   out.

1.

C   **Bb**

Lead: La - la - la   i   ka   la   ha - na - ha - na.

Chorus: Me   ke   kai   ho - en - e   i   ka   pu - 'e   one.

F   **N.C.**

Lead: He - le - he - le   mai   ka - kou   e.

Chorus: Ha - wai - ian   roll - er   coast - er   ride.

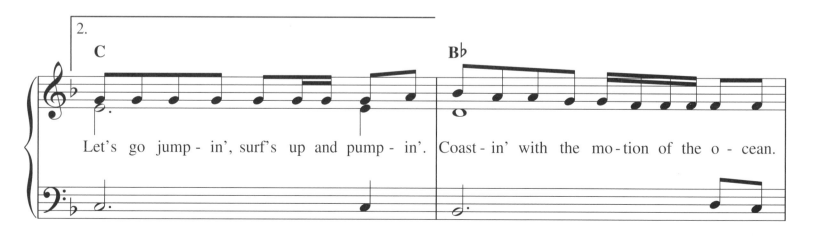

2.

C   **Bb**

Let's   go   jump - in',   surf's   up   and   pump - in'.   Coast - in'   with   the   mo - tion   of   the   o - cean.

F   **N.C.**

Whirl - pools swirl - ing, cas - cad - ing swirl - ing.

Chorus:
Ha - wai - ian roll - er coast - er ride.

F   **Gm**   **F**   **D.S. al Coda**   **Gm**

CODA   **C**   **B♭**

Lead:
La - la - la i ka la ha - na - ha - na.

Chorus:
Me ke kai ho - en - e i ka pu - 'e one.

F

Lead:
He - le - he - le mai ka - kou e.

Chorus:
Ha - wai - ian roll - er coast - er ride.

I JUST CAN'T WAIT TO BE KING

from Walt Disney Pictures' THE LION KING

Music by ELTON JOHN
Lyrics by TIM RICE

Simba: I'm gon-na be a might-y king, so

en - e - mies be - ware! *Zazu:* Well, I've nev - er seen a king of beasts with quite so lit - tle hair. *Simba:* I'm

gon - na be the mane e - vent, like no king was be -

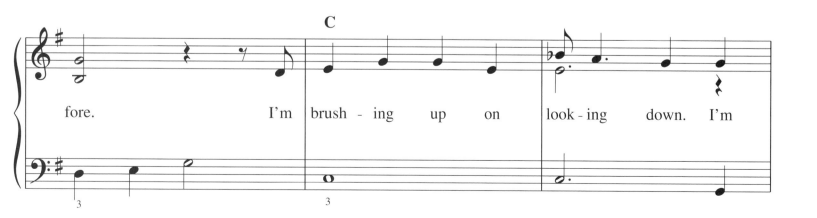

fore. I'm brush - ing up on look - ing down. I'm

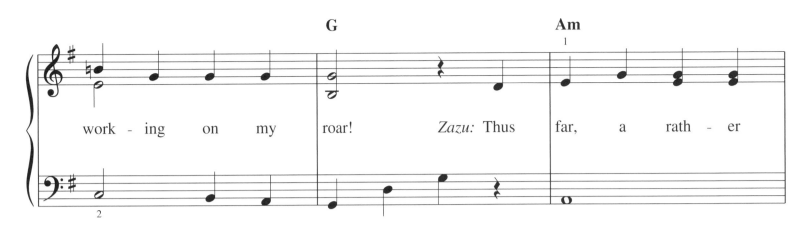

work - ing on my | roar! | *Zazu:* Thus | far, a rath - er

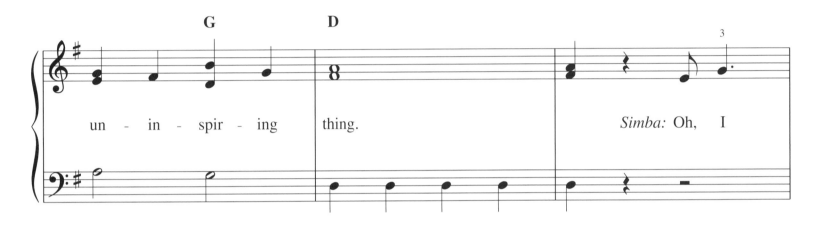

un - in - spir - ing | thing. | *Simba:* Oh, I

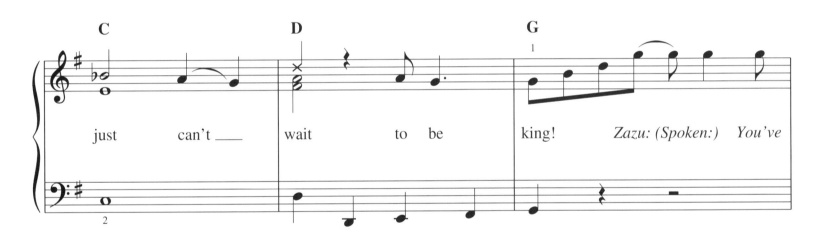

just can't ___ | wait to be | king! | *Zazu: (Spoken:)* You've

rather a long way to go, young | *Master! If you think...* | *Simba:* No one say - ing

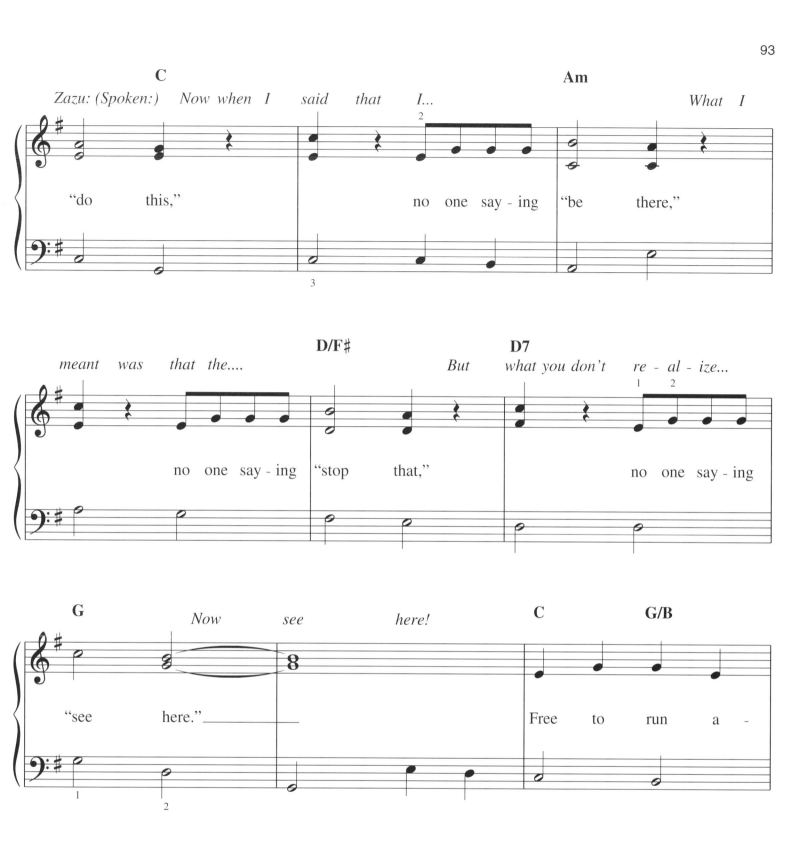

free to do it all my ___ way!

(Quasi spoken:)

Zazu: I think it's time that you and I ar -

(Sung:)

ranged a heart - to - heart. *Simba:* Kings don't need ad -

(Quasi spoken:)

vice from lit - tle horn - bills, for a start. *Zazu:* If

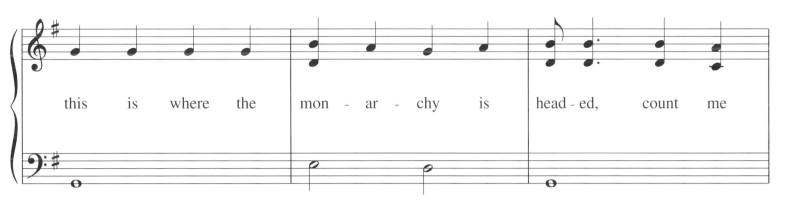

this is where the mon - ar - chy is head - ed, count me

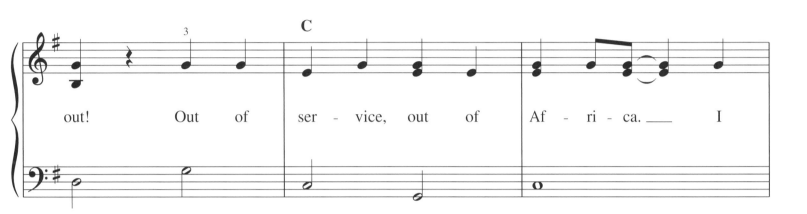

out! Out of ser - vice, out of Af - ri - ca.___ I

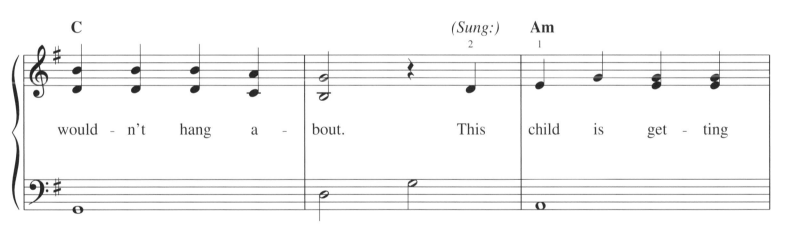

would - n't hang a - bout. This child is get - ting

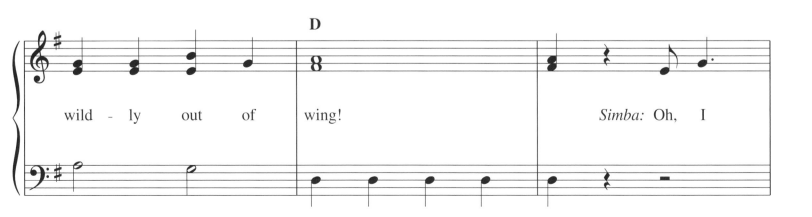

wild - ly out of wing! *Simba:* Oh, I

just   can't ___   wait   to   be   king!

Simba: Ev - 'ry - bod - y   look   left,

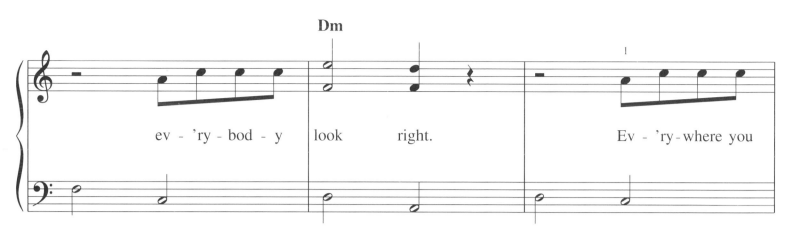

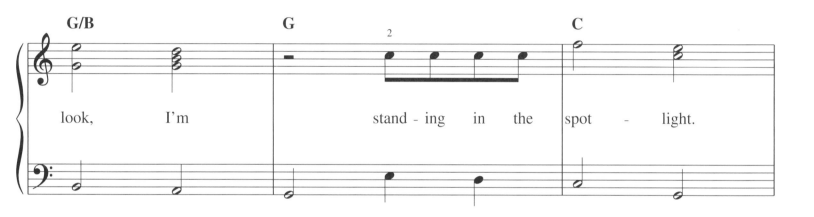

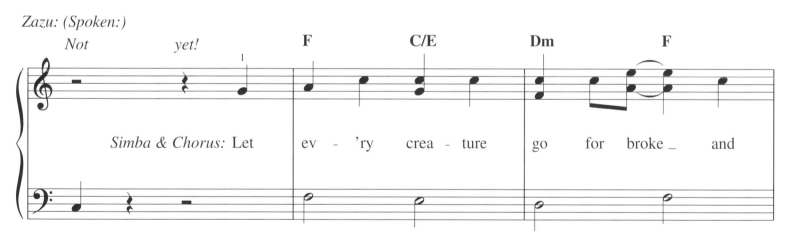

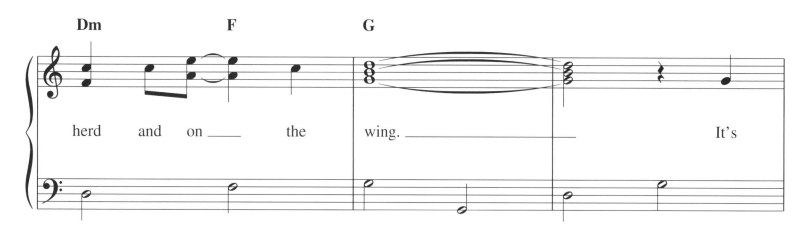

herd and on _____ the wing. _____ It's

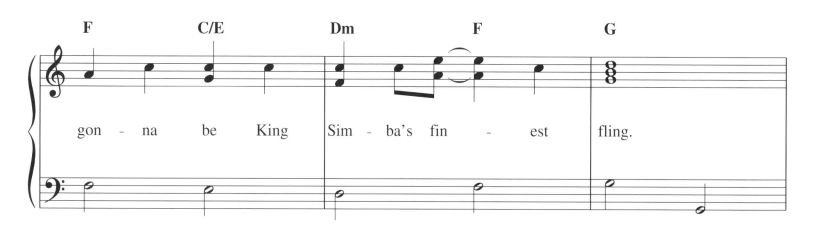

gon - na be King Sim - ba's fin - est fling.

Simba: Oh, I just can't _____ wait to be

king. Oh, I just can't _____

IF I DIDN'T HAVE YOU

from Walt Disney Pictures Presents A Pixar Animation Studios Film MONSTERS, INC.

Music and Lyrics by
RANDY NEWMAN

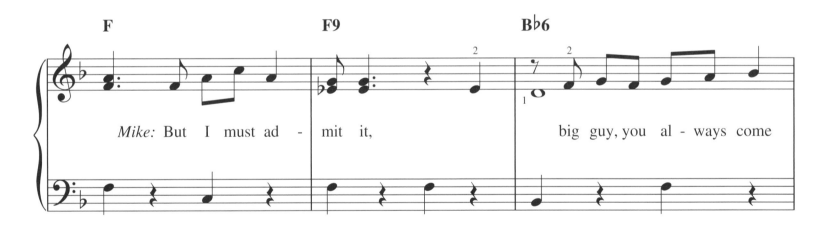

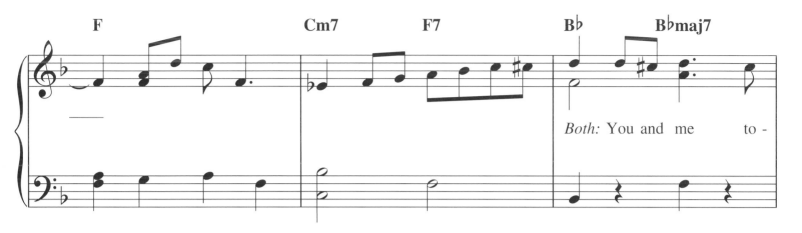

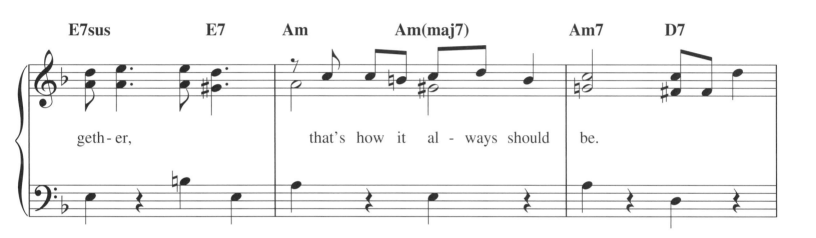

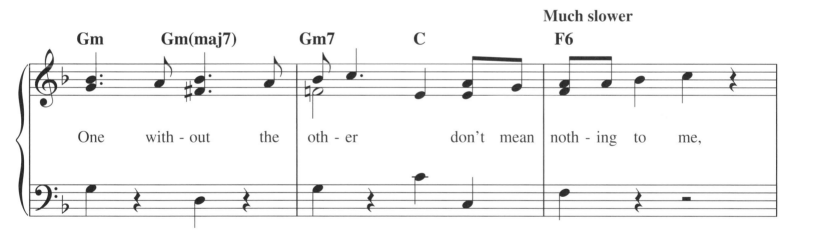

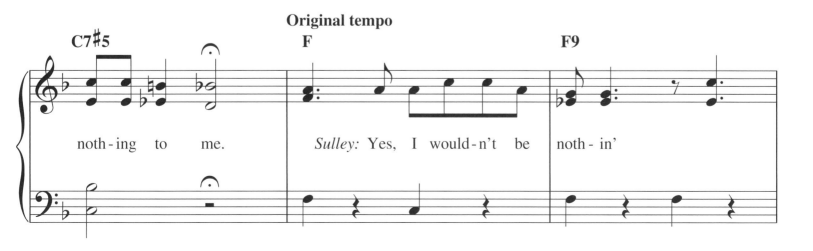

B♭6 | **B♭m6** | **F**

Sulley:

if I did-n't have you ___ I would-n't know where to

Mike: I know what you mean, *Sulley, because...*

D7 | **G9** | **C7sus**

go would-n't know what to do.

Mike: Me too, because I... *Mike:* *Why do you keep singing my part?*

F | **F9** | **B♭6**

Both: I don't have to say it *Both:* both know it's true. ___

Sulley: I'll say it anyway. *Mike: 'Cause we*

B♭m6 | **F** | **D7** | **G9** | **C7sus**

___ I would-n't have noth-in' if I did-n't have,

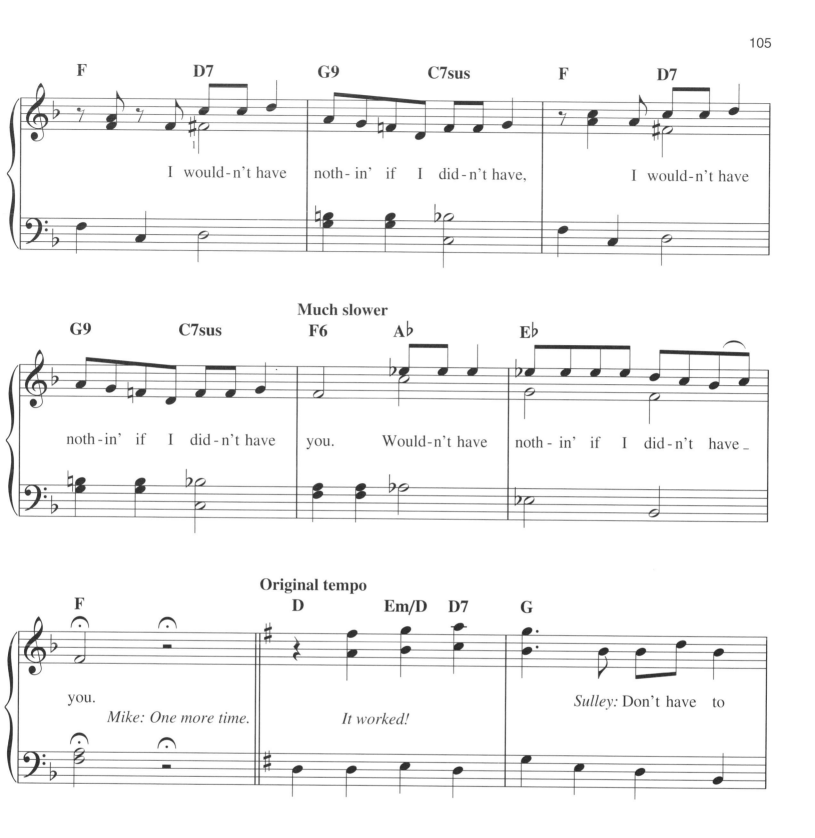

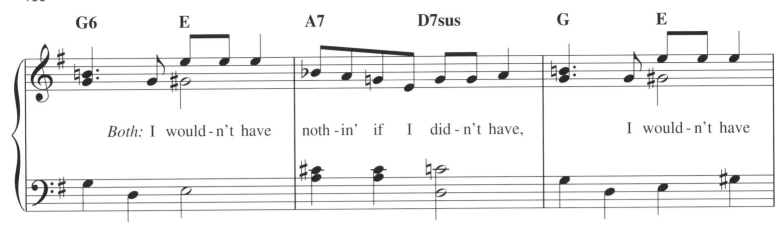

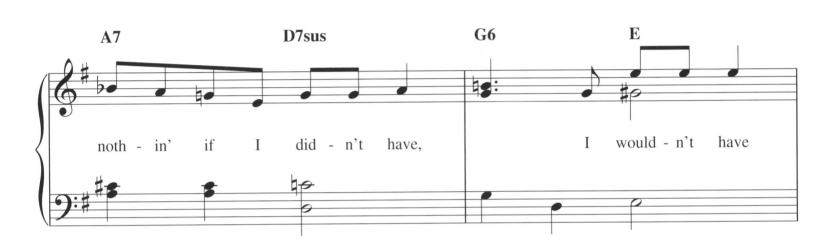

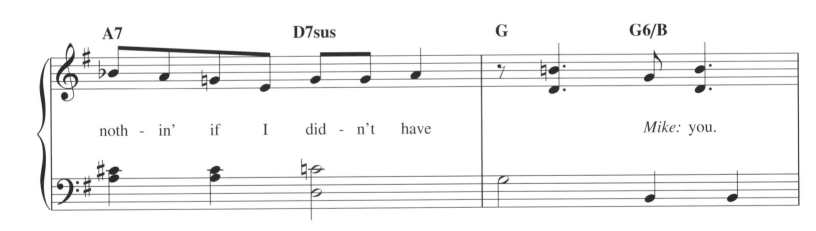

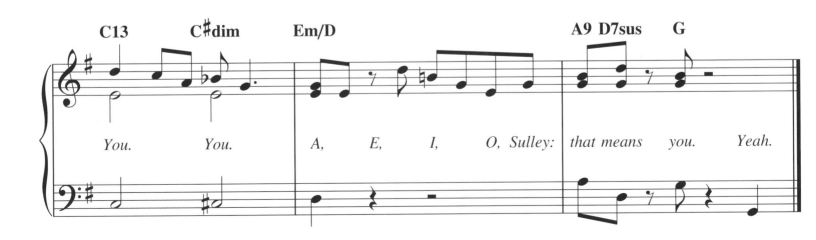

THE INCREDITS
from Walt Disney Pictures' THE INCREDIBLES - A Pixar Film

Music by
MICHAEL GIACCHINO

IF I NEVER KNEW YOU

(Love Theme from POCAHONTAS)
from Walt Disney's POCAHONTAS

Music by ALAN MENKEN
Lyrics by STEPHEN SCHWARTZ

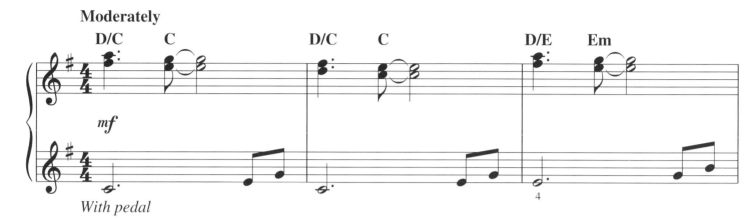

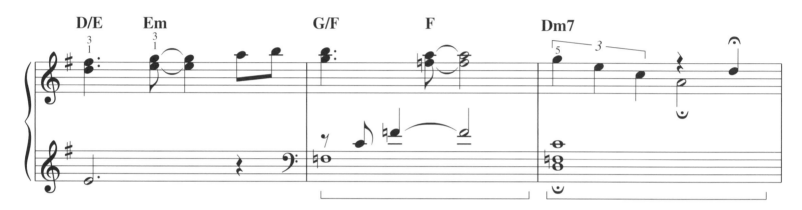

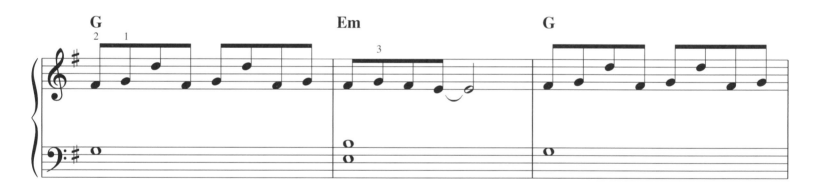

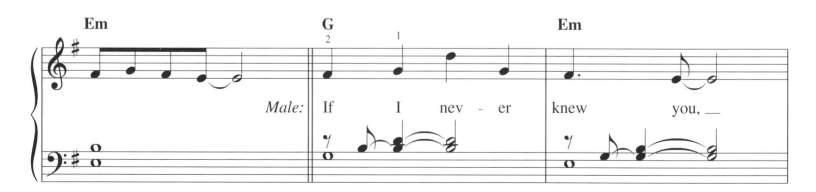

Male: If I nev-er knew you, ___

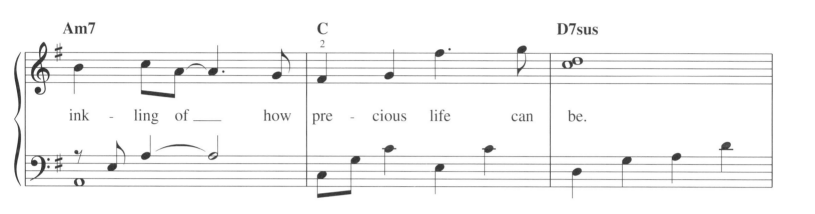

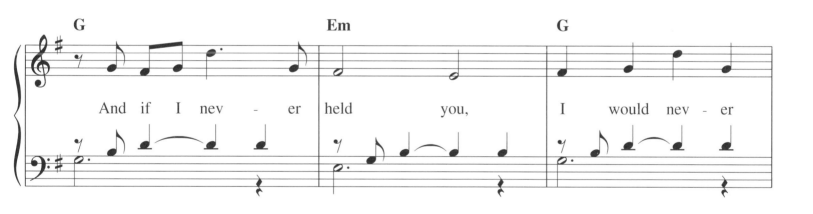

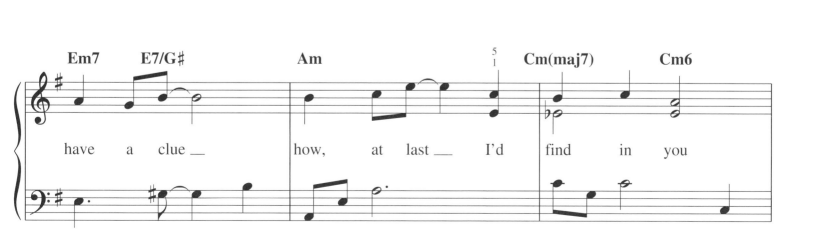

the miss-ing part of me. _____ In this world so

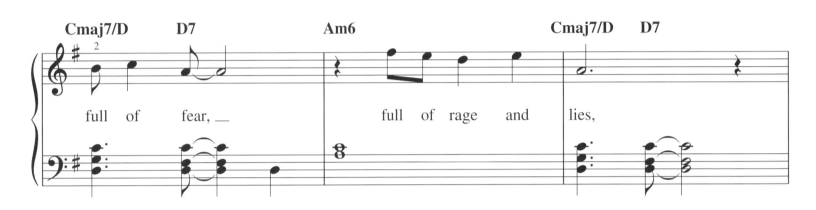

full of fear, __ full of rage and lies,

I can see __ the truth so clear __ in your eyes, __ so

dry your eyes. __ And I'm so grate - ful to you.

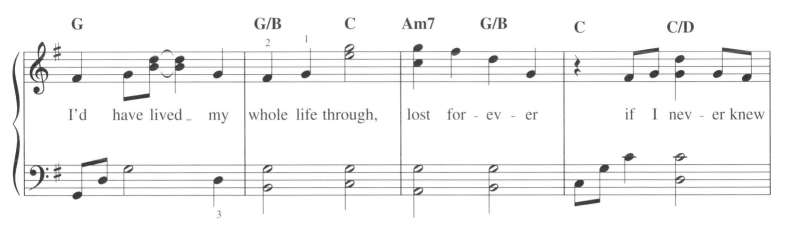

I'd have lived _ my whole life through, lost for - ev - er if I nev - er knew

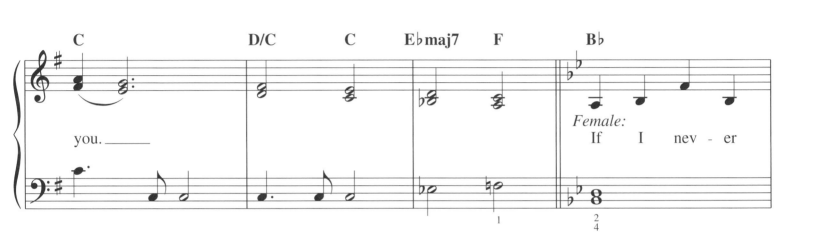

you. _____

Female:
If I nev - er

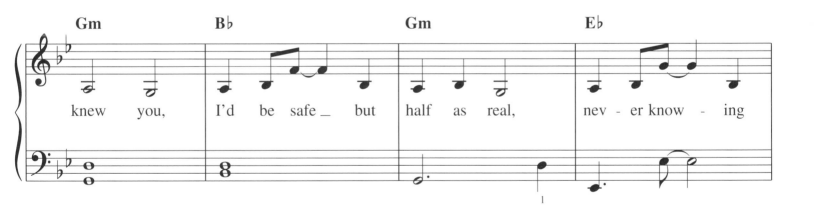

knew you, I'd be safe _ but half as real, nev - er know - ing

I could feel _ a love so strong and true. I'm so grate - ful

Gm   **Bb**   **Bb/D**   **Eb**   **Cm7**   **Bb/D**

to   you.   I'd   have   lived _ my   whole   life through,   lost   for - ev - er

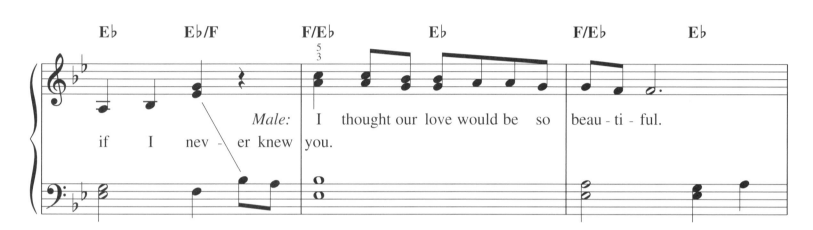

Eb   **Eb/F**   **F/Eb**   **Eb**   **F/Eb**   **Eb**

if   I   nev - er knew you.   *Male:*   I   thought our love would be   so   beau - ti - ful.

Dm7   **Gm**

Female: Some - how we'd make the whole world   bright. _   *Both:*   I   nev - er knew that fear and

Ebmaj7   **Bb/D**   **Gm**   **Dm7**   **Eb**

hate could be   so strong,   all they'd leave us were these whis-pers in the   night, ___   but

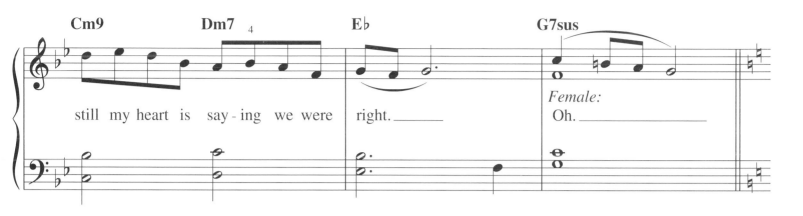

Cm9   Dm7   Eb   G7sus

still my heart is say-ing we were right._____

Female:
Oh._____

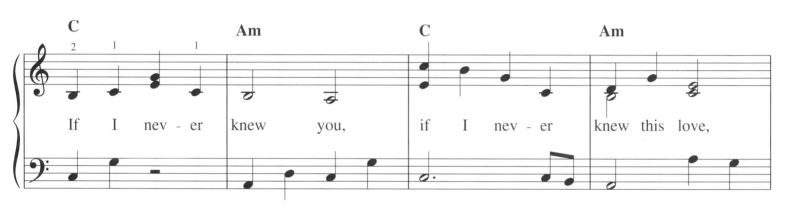

C   Am   C   Am

If I nev - er knew you, if I nev - er knew this love,

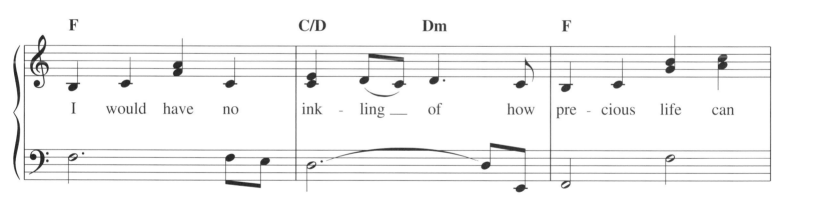

F   C/D   Dm   F

I would have no ink - ling ___ of how pre - cious life can

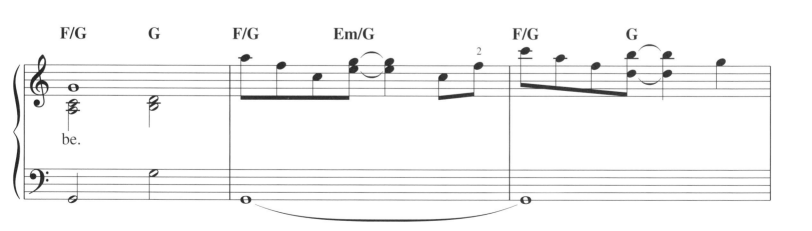

F/G   G   F/G   Em/G   F/G   G

be.

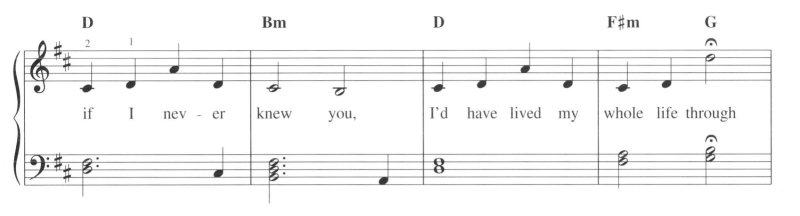

if I nev - er knew you, I'd have lived my whole life through

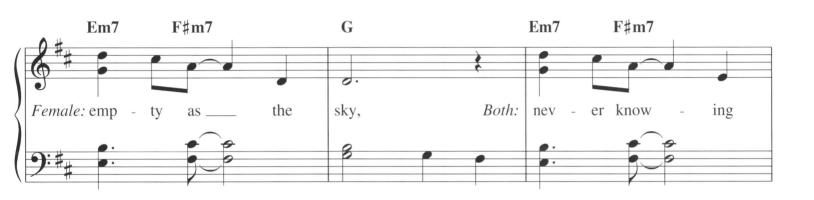

Female: emp - ty as ___ the sky, *Both:* nev - er know - ing

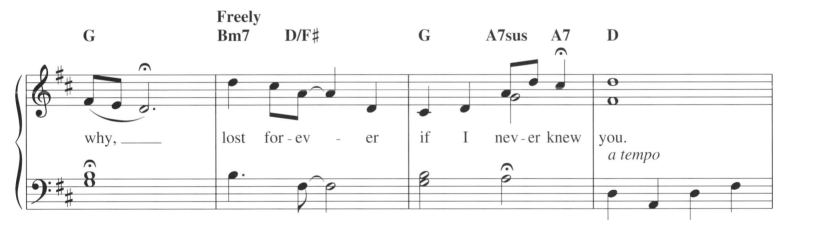

Freely

why, ___ lost for - ev - er if I nev - er knew you.

a tempo

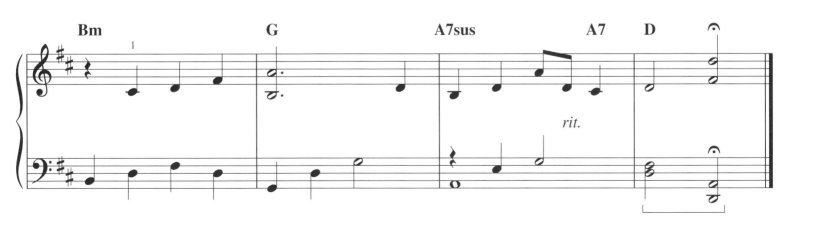

rit.

JUST AROUND THE RIVERBEND

from Walt Disney's POCAHONTAS

Music by ALAN MENKEN
Lyrics by STEPHEN SCHWARTZ

all must pay a price: To be safe we lose our chance of ev - er

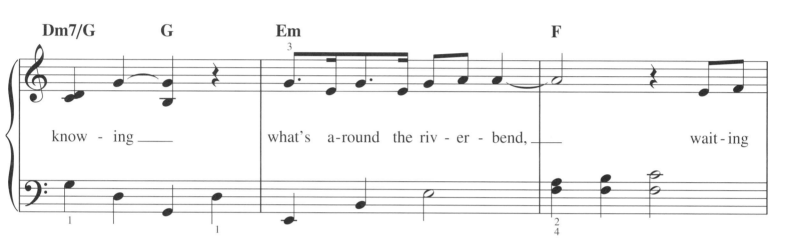

know - ing _____ what's a-round the riv - er - bend, _____ wait - ing

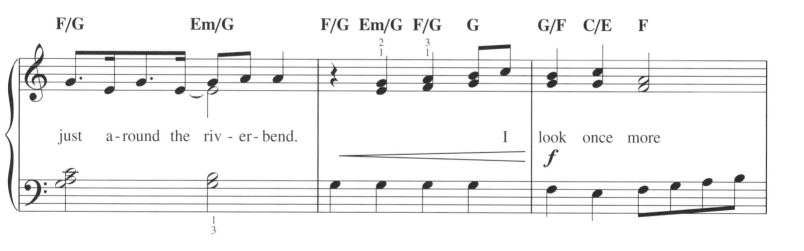

just a-round the riv - er - bend. I look once more

just a-round the riv - er - bend be - yond the shore, where the gulls fly free. Don't

know what for, what I dream the day might send just a-round the riv - er - bend _

_ for me, _ com - ing for

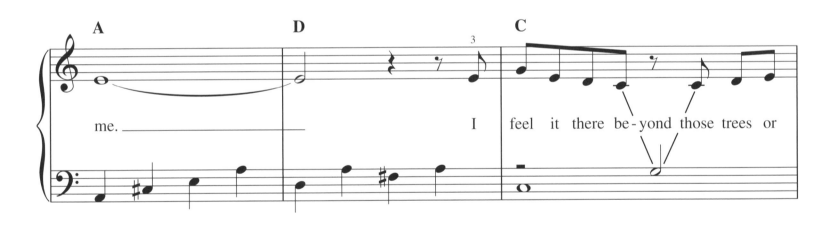

me. _ I feel it there be - yond those trees or

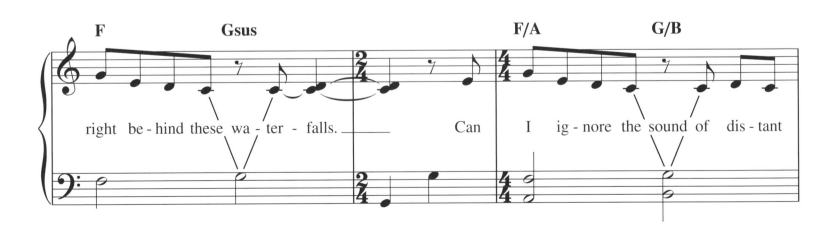

right be - hind these wa - ter - falls. _ Can I ig - nore the sound of dis - tant

drum-ming for a hand-some stur-dy hus-band who builds hand-some stur-dy walls and

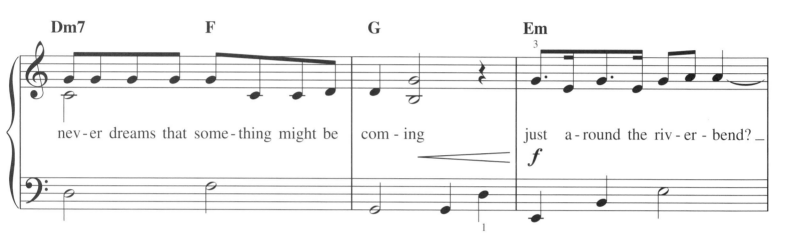

nev-er dreams that some-thing might be com-ing just a-round the riv-er-bend? __

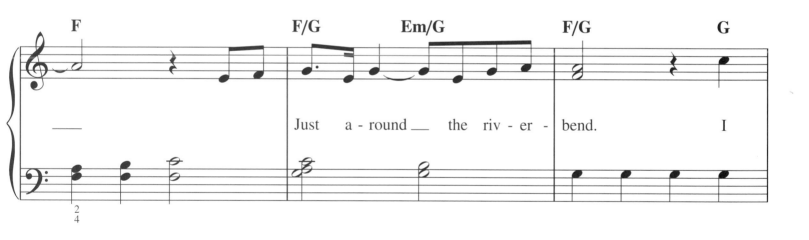

__ Just a-round __ the riv-er- bend. I

look once more just a-round the riv-er-bend be-yond the shore,

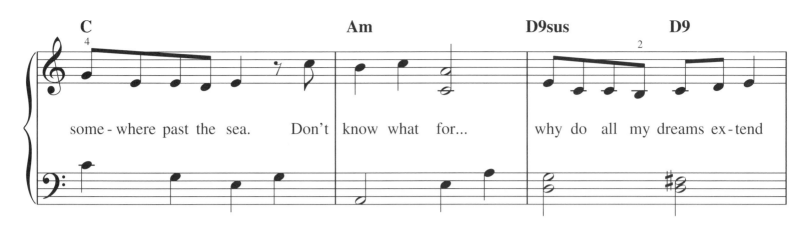

C   Am   D9sus   D9

some-where past the sea.   Don't know what for...   why do all my dreams ex-tend

F/G   F+/G   Dm/G

just   a-round the riv - er - bend? ___   Just   a - round __ the riv - er -

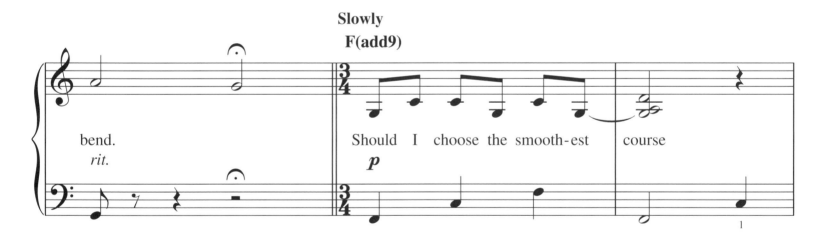

Slowly
F(add9)

bend.   Should I choose the smooth-est   course
rit.   **p**

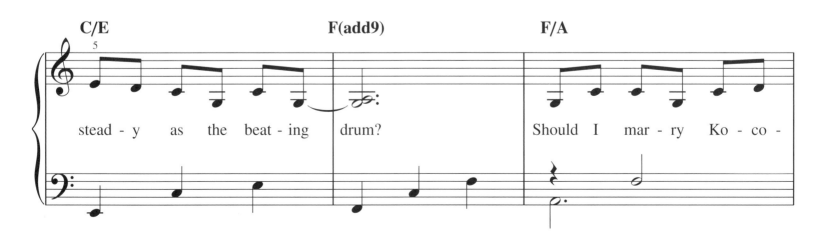

C/E   F(add9)   F/A

stead - y as the beat - ing drum?   Should I mar - ry Ko - co -

um? _____ Is all my dream-ing at an end? Or

do you still wait for me, ___ Dream Giv - er _____

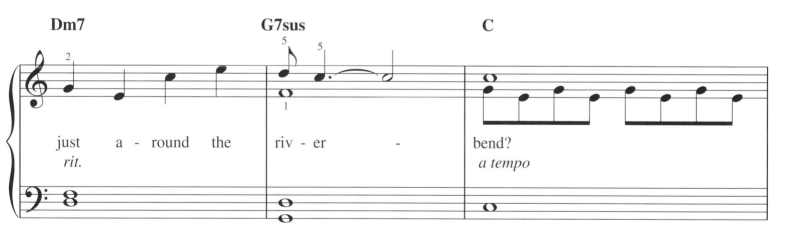

just a - round the riv - er - bend?

rit. *a tempo*

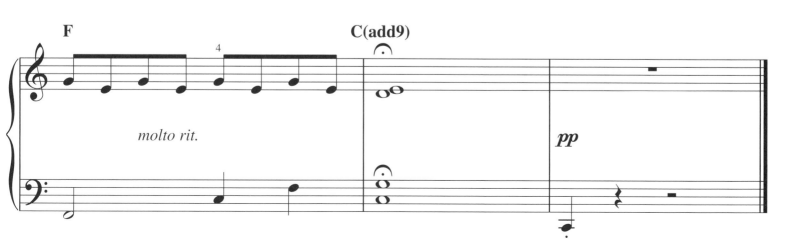

molto rit. ***pp***

KISS THE GIRL

from Walt Disney's THE LITTLE MERMAID

Lyrics by HOWARD ASHMAN
Music by ALAN MENKEN

There you see her sit-ting there a-cross the

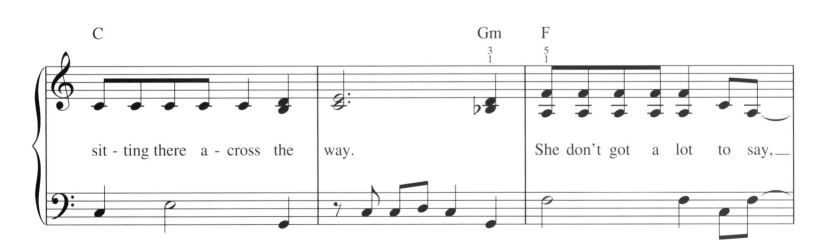

way. She don't got a lot to say,

but there's some - thing a - bout her.

And you

don't know why,___ but you're dy - ing to try. You wan - na

kiss the girl.

Yes, you want her.

Look at her, you know you do.

Pos - si - ble she wants you, too.___

There is one way to ask her. It don't

take a word,___ not a sin - gle word,___ go on and kiss the girl.

Sha la la la la la, my oh my,___ look like the

boy too shy.___ Ain't gon - na kiss the girl. Sha la la la la la,

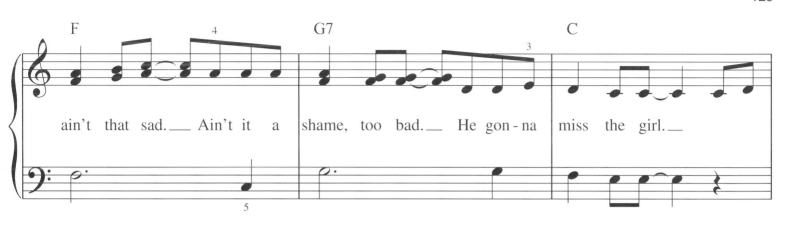

ain't that sad.__ Ain't it a shame, too bad.__ He gon-na miss the girl.__

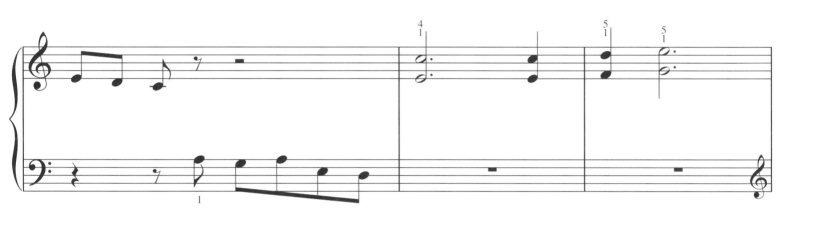

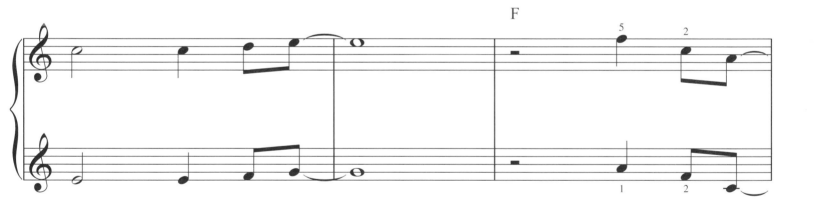

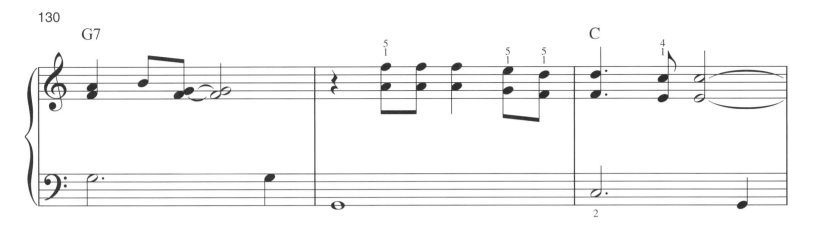

Now's　　　your　mo - ment,　　　　float - ing　in　a　blue　la -

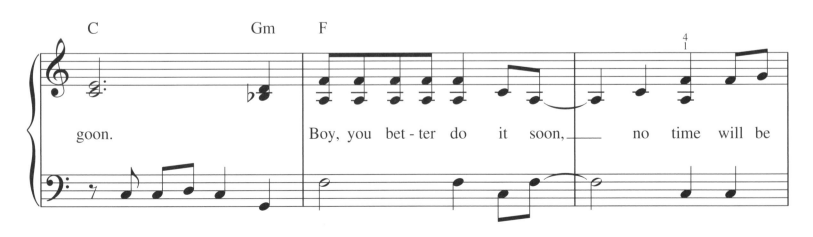

goon.　　　　　　Boy, you　bet - ter　do　it　soon,＿＿　no　time　will　be

THE MEDALLION CALLS

from Walt Disney Pictures' PIRATES OF THE CARIBBEAN: THE CURSE OF THE BLACK PEARL

Music by KLAUS BADELT

LES POISSONS

from Walt Disney's THE LITTLE MERMAID

Music by ALAN MENKEN
Lyrics by HOWARD ASHMAN

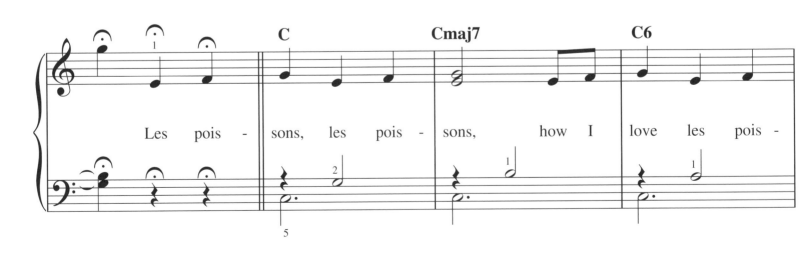

Les pois - sons, les pois - sons, how I love les pois -

sons, love to chop and to serve lit - tle fish. _____

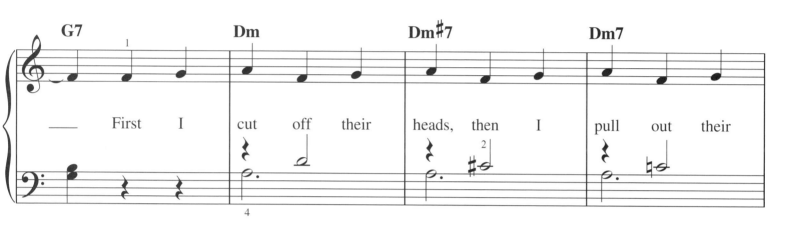

_____ First I cut off their heads, then I pull out their

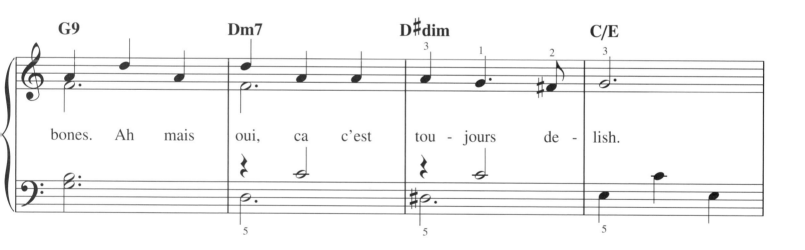

bones. Ah mais oui, ca c'est tou - jours de - lish.

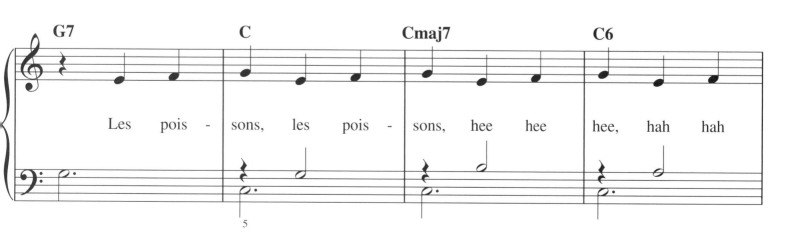

Les pois - sons, les pois - sons, hee hee hee, hah hah

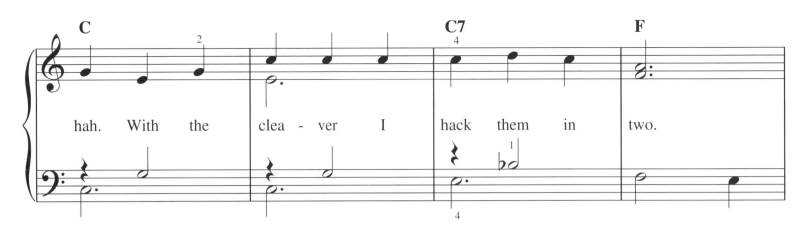

hah. With the cleaver I hack them in two.

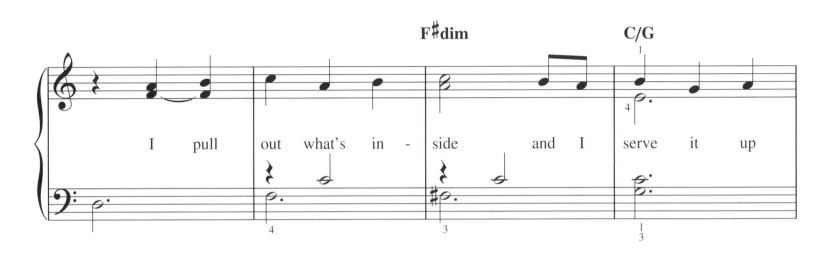

I pull out what's in - side and I serve it up

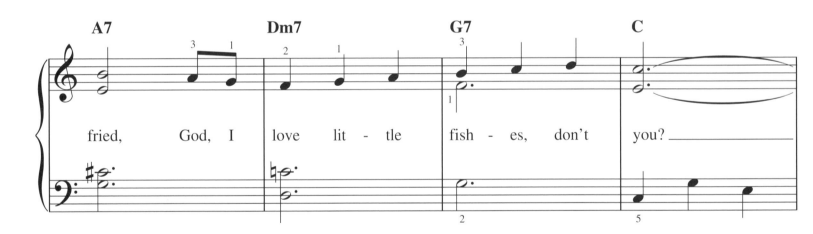

fried, God, I love lit - tle fish - es, don't you? _____

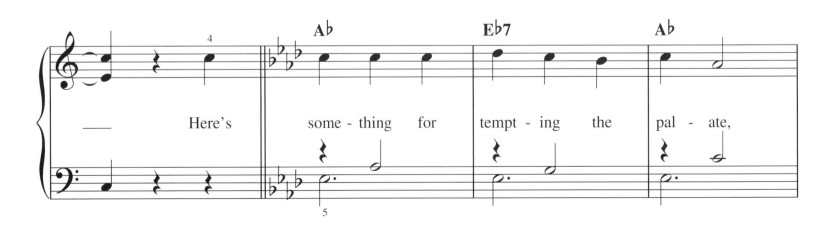

_____ Here's some - thing for tempt - ing the pal - ate,

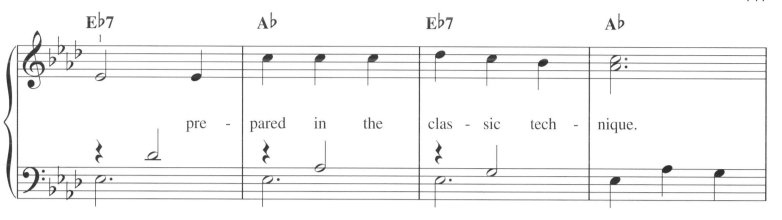

pre - pared in the clas - sic tech - nique.

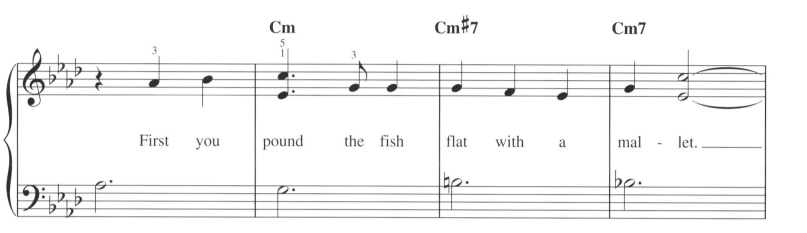

First you pound the fish flat with a mal - let.

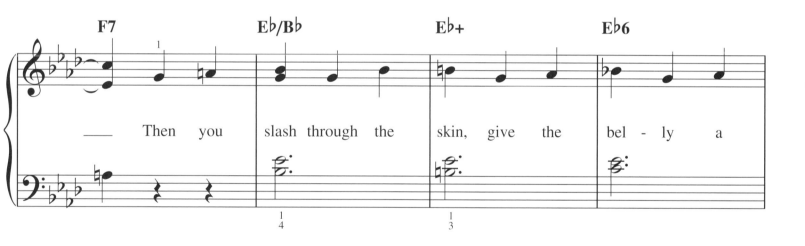

Then you slash through the skin, give the bel - ly a

slice, then you rub some salt in 'cause that makes it taste

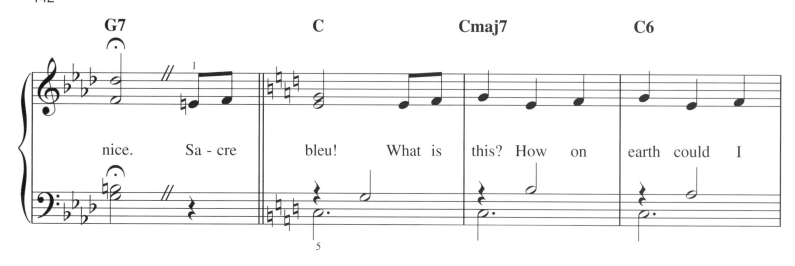

nice. Sa - cre bleu! What is this? How on earth could I

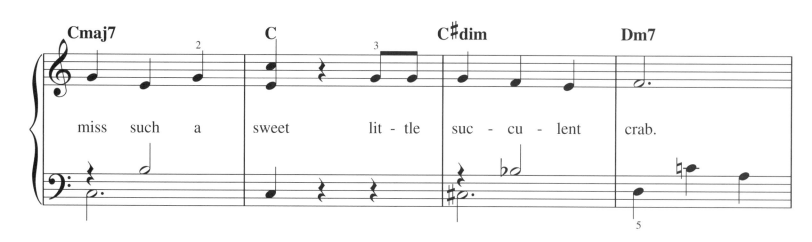

miss such a sweet lit - tle suc - cu - lent crab.

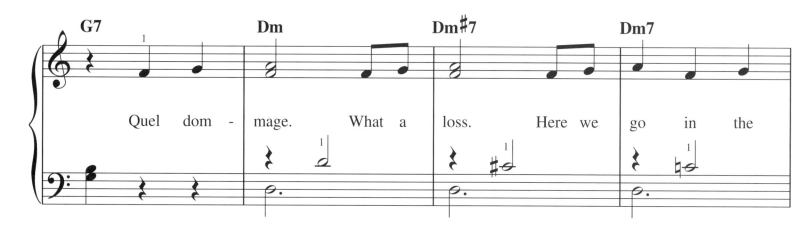

Quel dom - mage. What a loss. Here we go in the

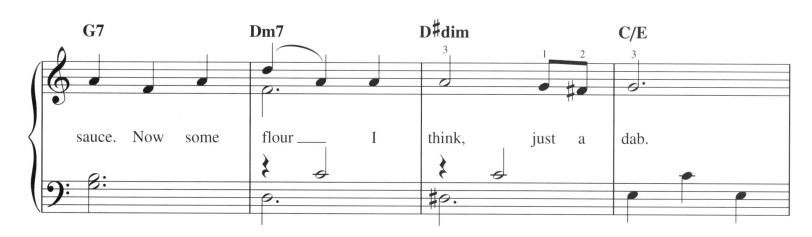

sauce. Now some flour ____ I think, just a dab.

G7 | **C** | **Cmaj7** | **C6**

Now I stuff you with bread. It don't hurt 'cause you're

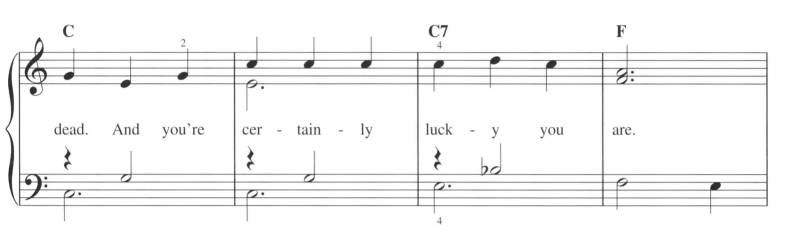

C | | **C7** | **F**

dead. And you're cer - tain - ly luck - y you are.

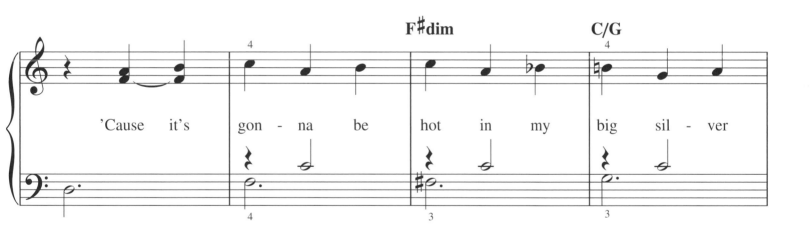

| | **F♯dim** | **C/G**

'Cause it's gon - na be hot in my big sil - ver

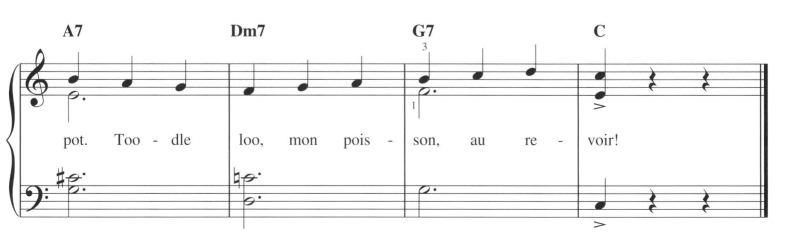

A7 | **Dm7** | **G7** | **C**

pot. Too - dle loo, mon pois - son, au re - voir!

LOOK THROUGH MY EYES

from Walt Disney Pictures' BROTHER BEAR

Words and Music by
PHIL COLLINS

Moderately, in 1

There are things in _____
There will be in times_

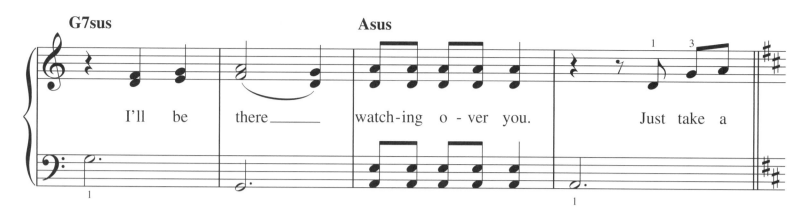

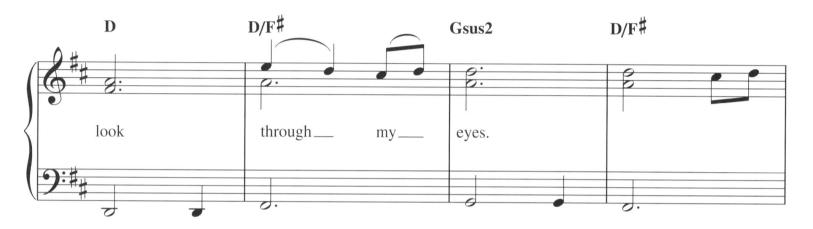

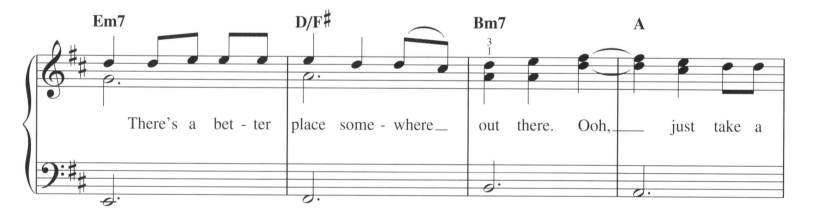

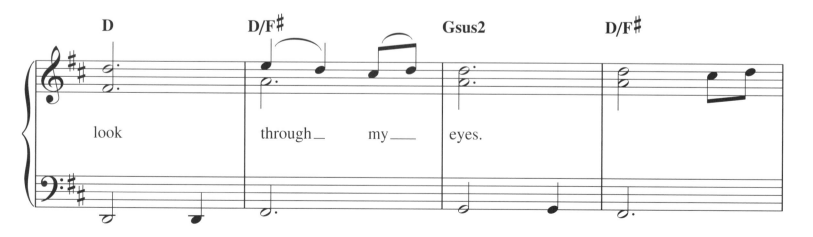

Ev -'ry -thing chang - es; you'll be a - mazed what you'll

find if you look through my___

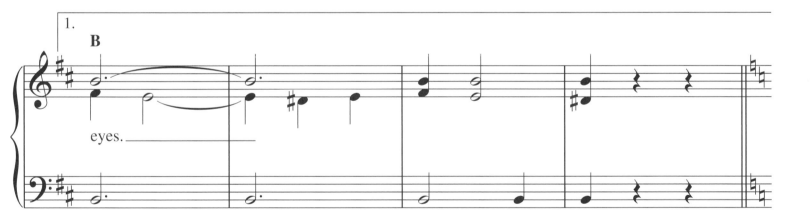

eyes.____

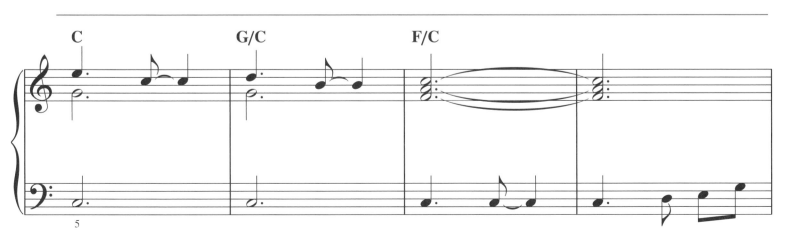

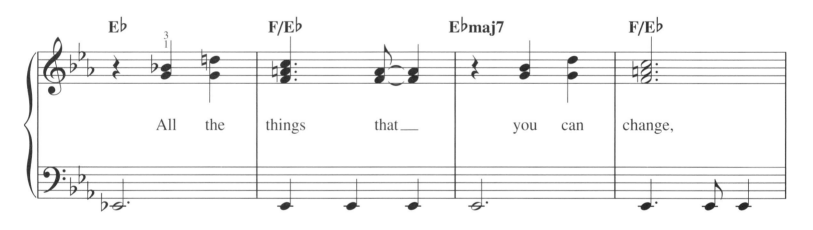

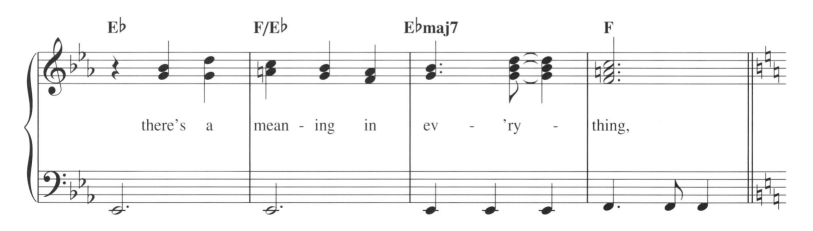

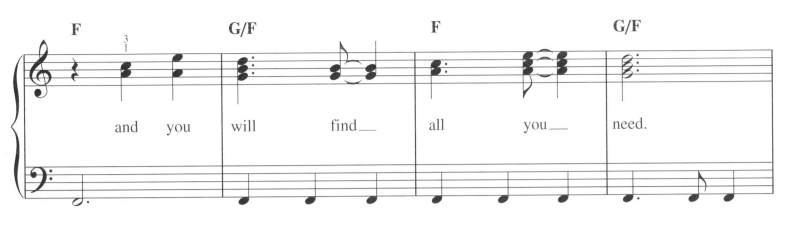

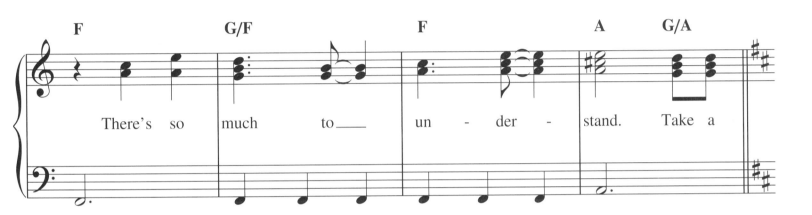

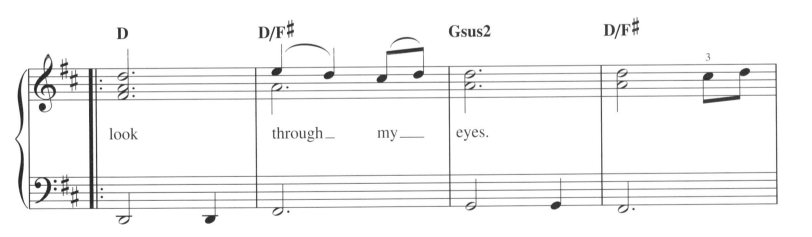

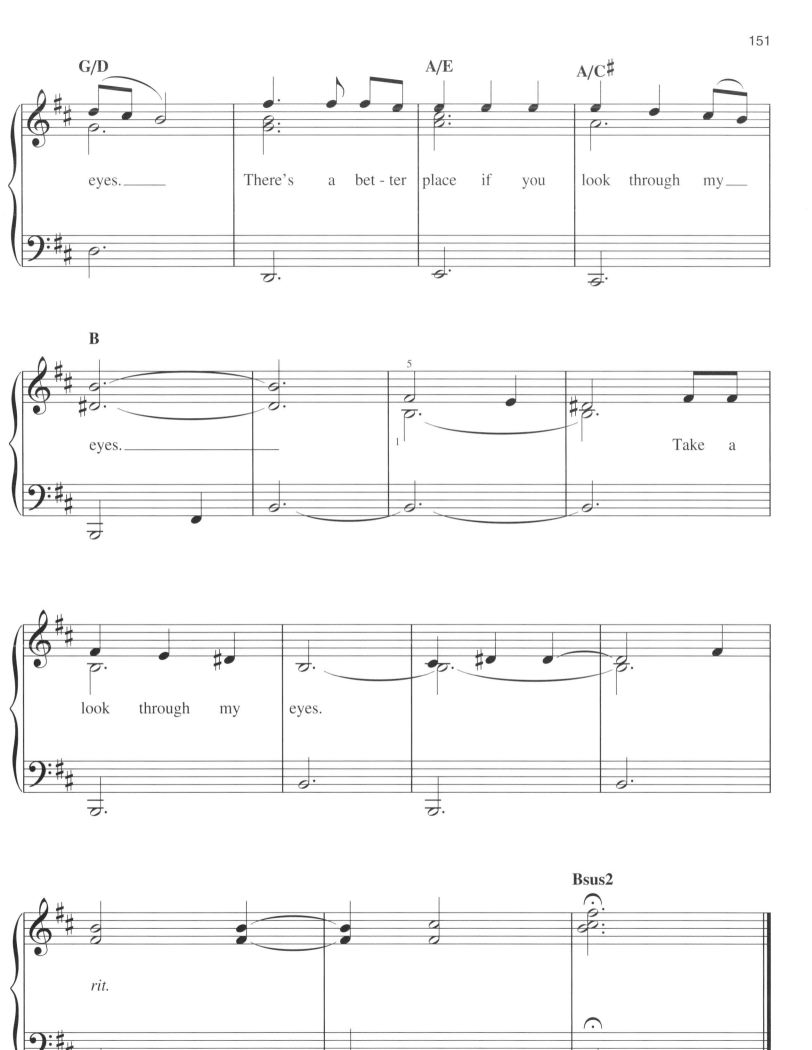

MY FUNNY FRIEND AND ME

from Walt Disney Pictures' THE EMPEROR'S NEW GROOVE

Lyrics by STING
Music by STING and DAVID HARTLEY

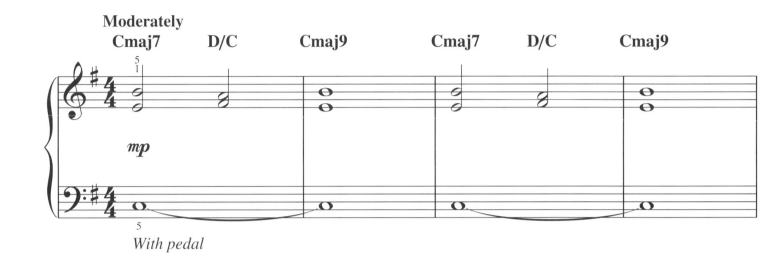

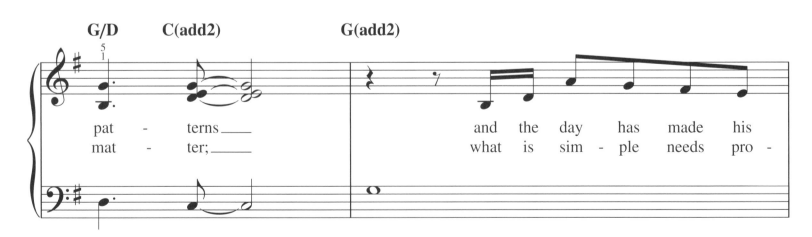

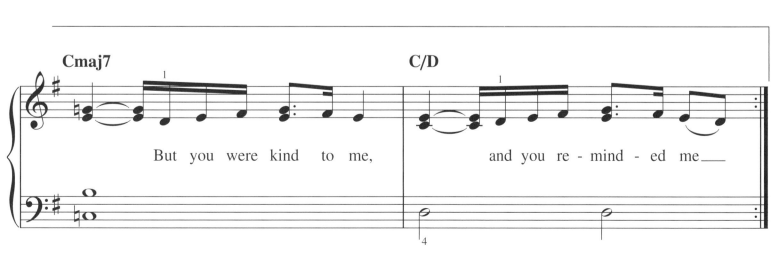

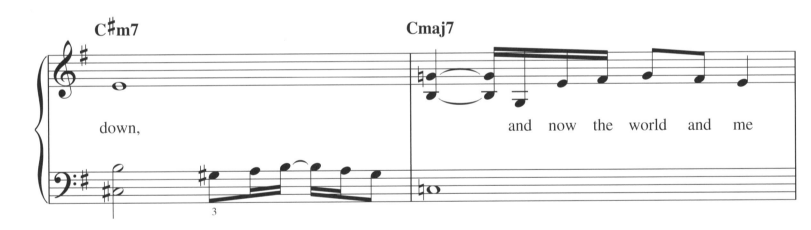

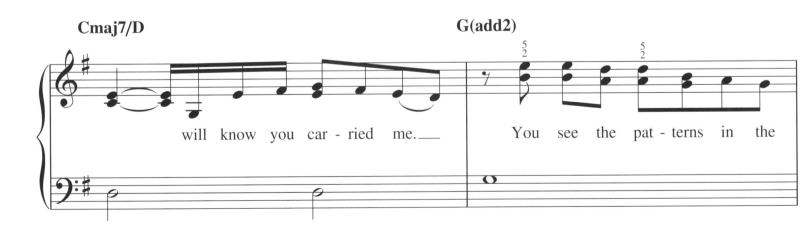

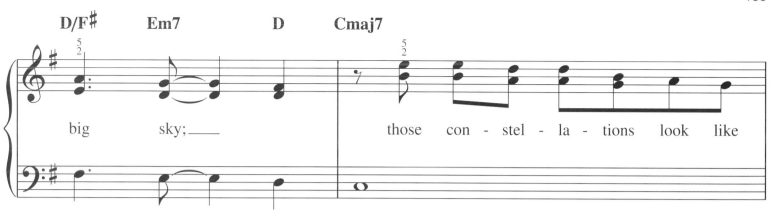

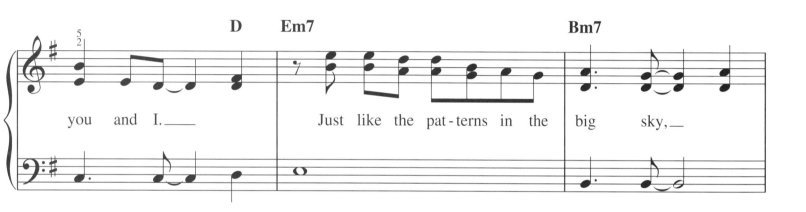

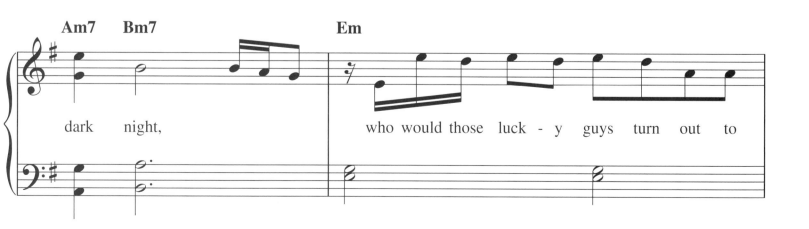

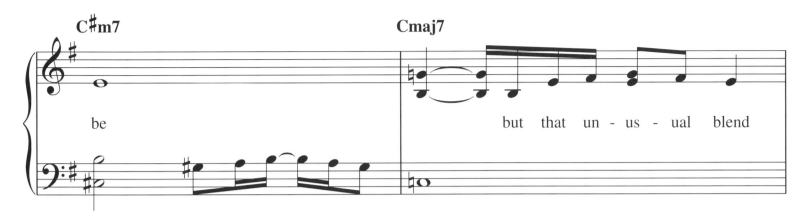

be

but that un - us - ual blend

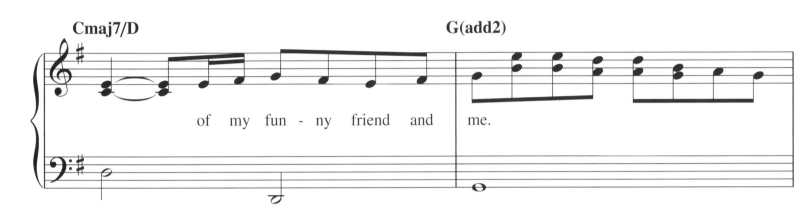

of my fun - ny friend and me.

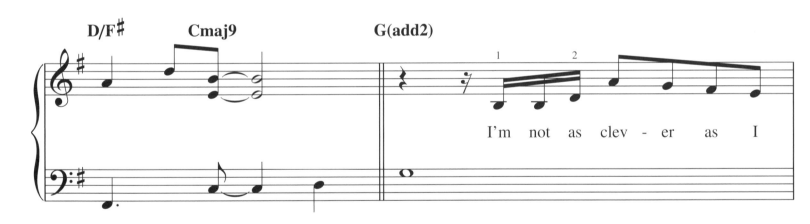

I'm not as clev - er as I

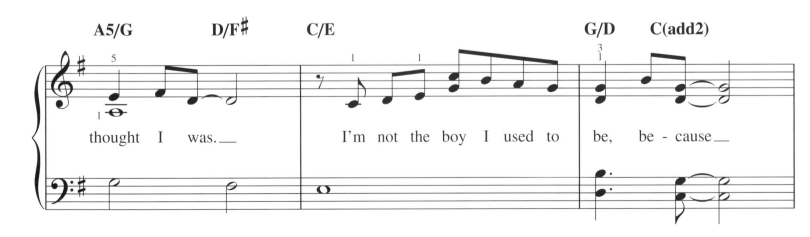

thought I was. ___ I'm not the boy I used to be, be - cause___

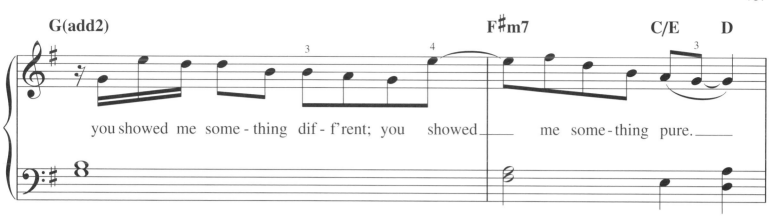

you showed me some - thing dif - f'rent; you showed____ me some - thing pure.____

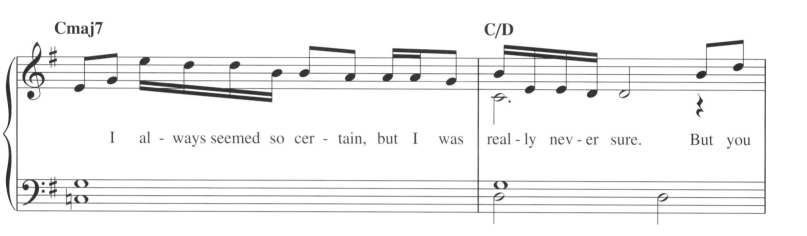

I al - ways seemed so cer - tain, but I was real - ly nev - er sure. But you

stayed,_____ and you called my name____

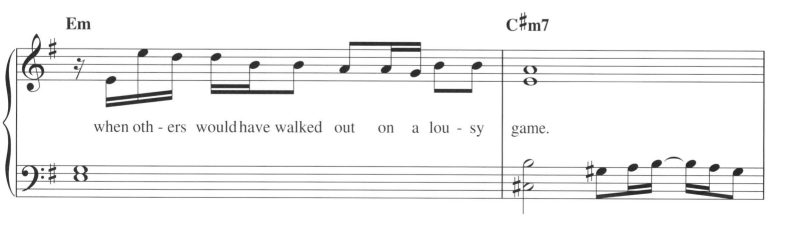

when oth - ers would have walked out on a lou - sy game.

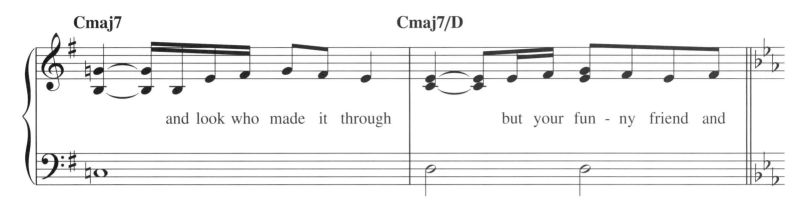

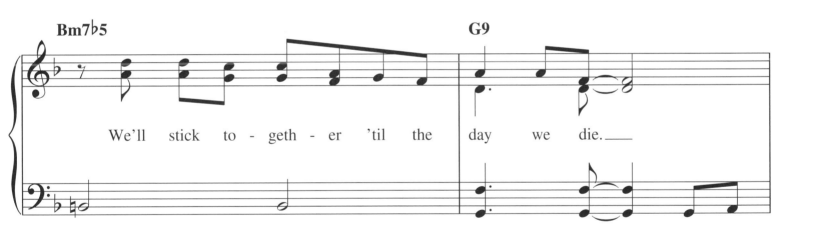

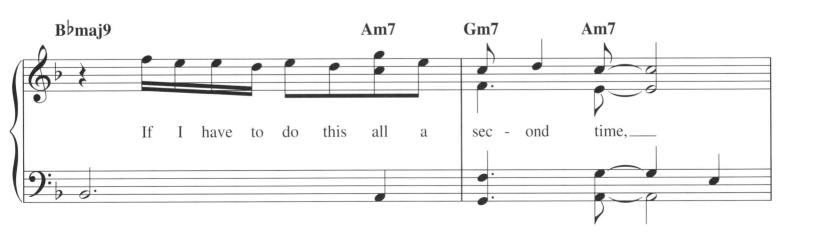

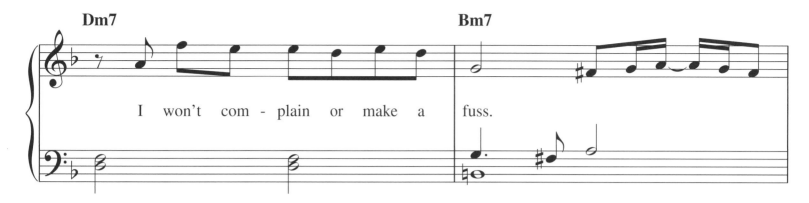

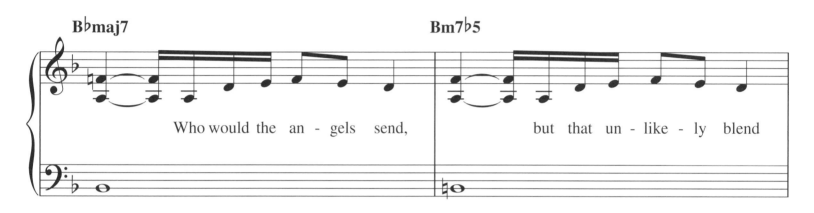

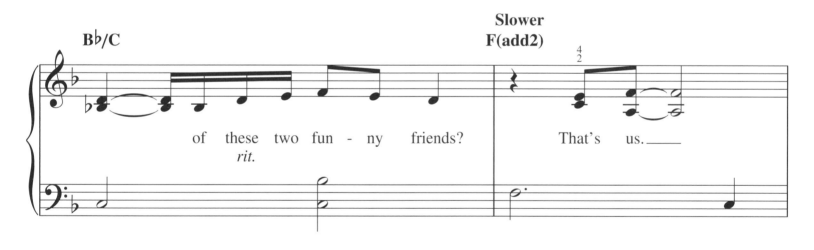

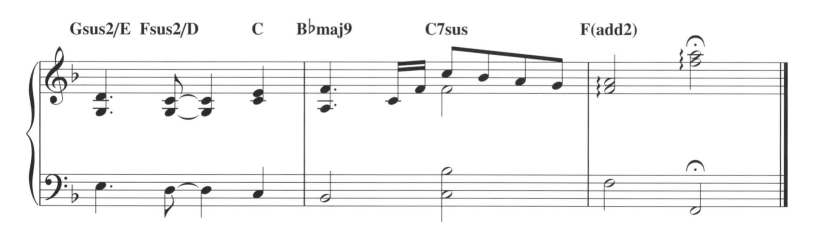

PART OF YOUR WORLD

from Walt Disney's THE LITTLE MERMAID

Music by ALAN MENKEN
Lyrics by HOWARD ASHMAN

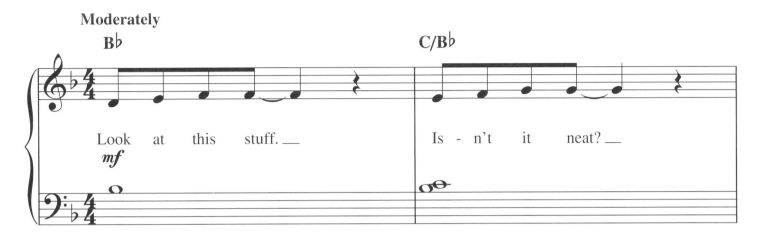

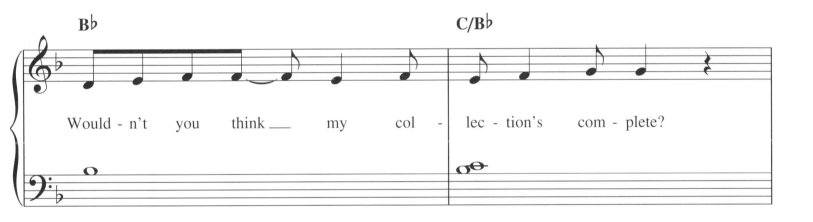

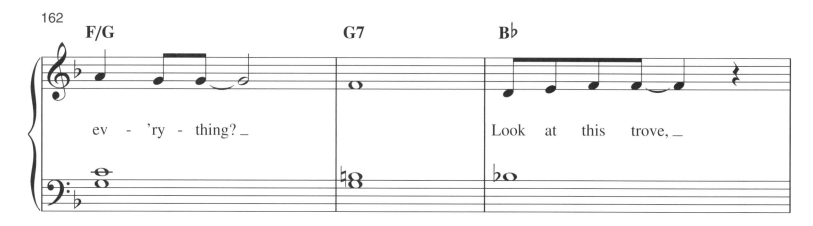

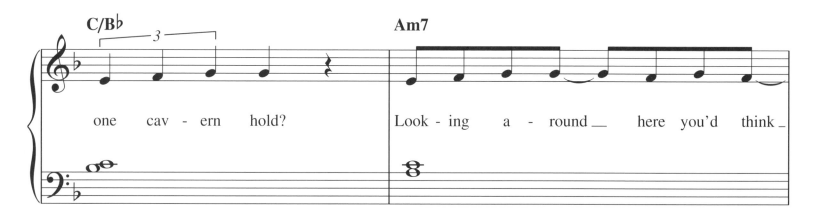

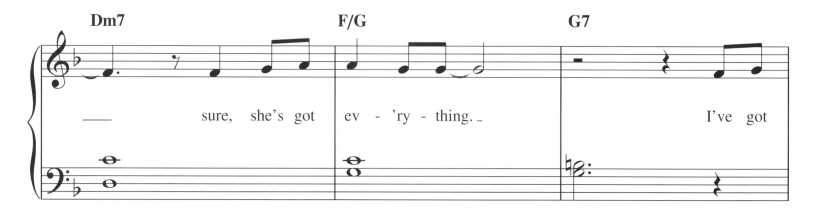

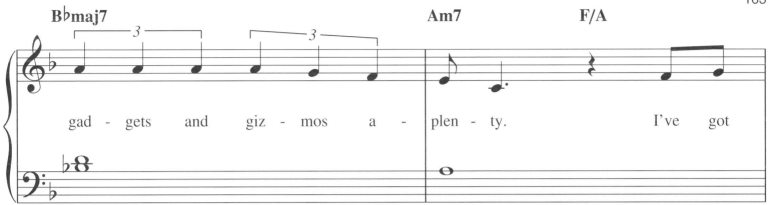

gad - gets and giz - mos a - plen - ty. I've got

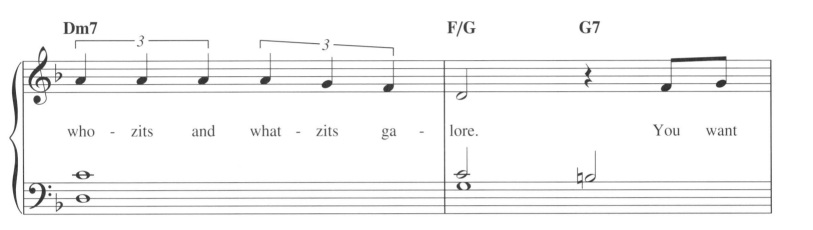

who - zits and what - zits ga - lore. You want

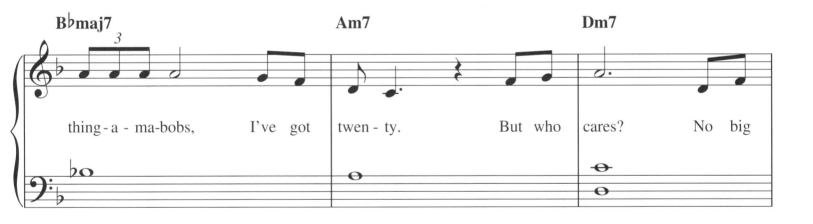

thing-a-ma-bobs, I've got twen - ty. But who cares? No big

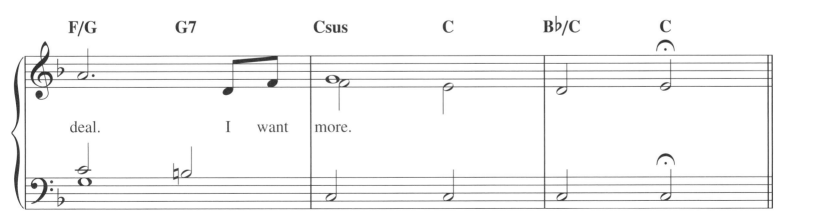

deal. I want more.

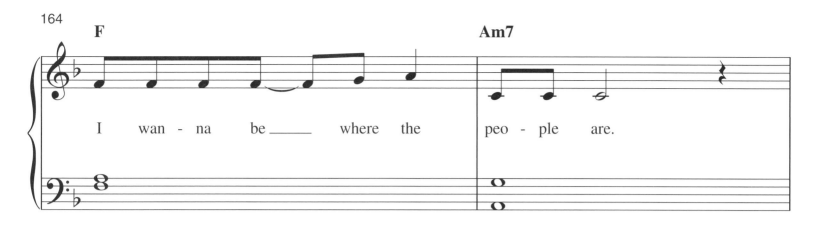

I wan - na be ____ where the peo - ple are.

I wan - na see ____ wan - na see 'em danc - in',

walk - in' a - round ____ on those, what - d - ya call ____ 'em, oh

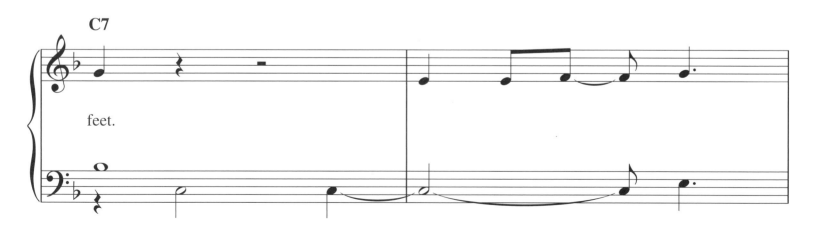

feet.

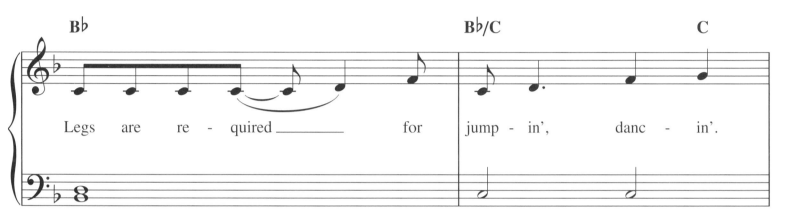

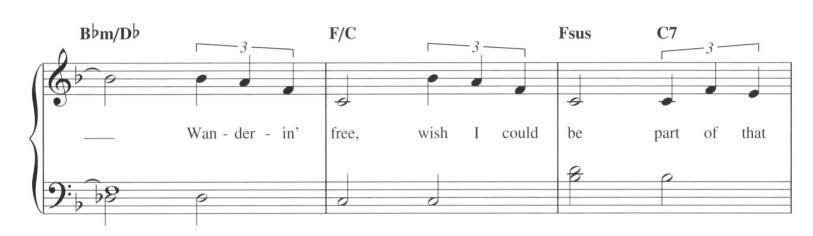

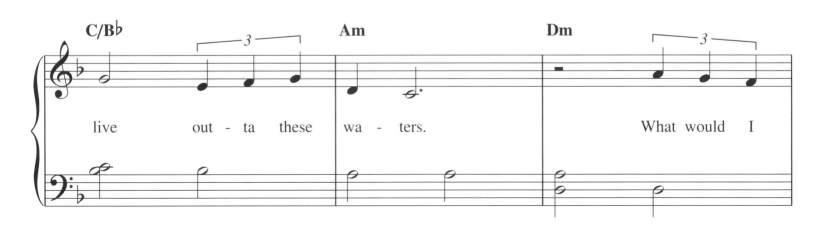

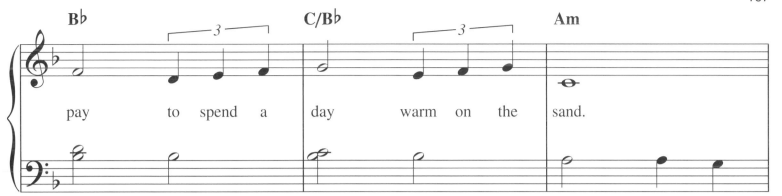

pay   to spend a   day   warm on the   sand.

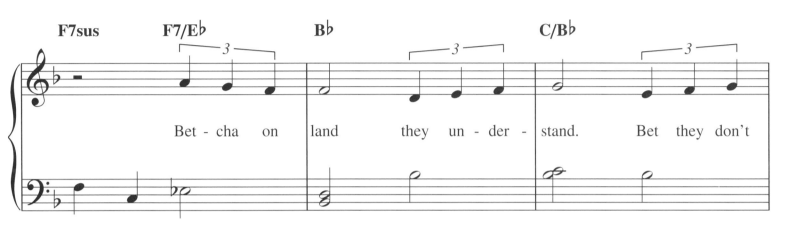

Bet - cha on   land   they un - der - stand.   Bet they don't

rep - ri - mand___   their daugh   - ters.   Bright young

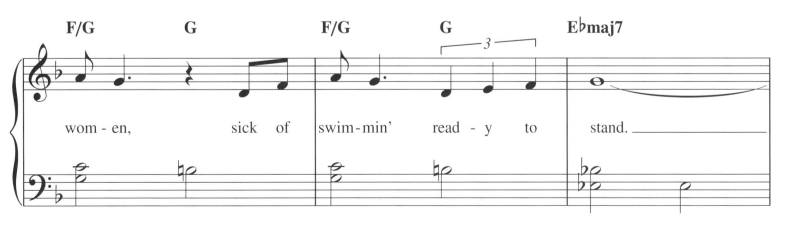

wom - en,   sick of   swim-min'   read - y to   stand. ___

And read - y to know ___ what the

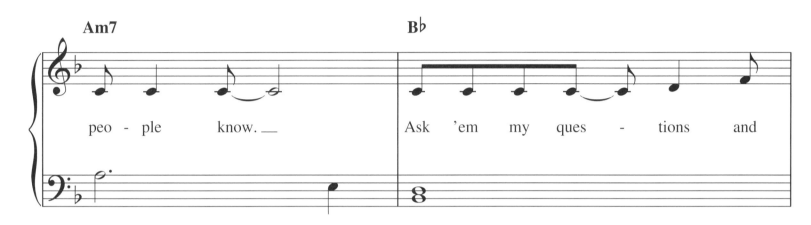

peo - ple know. ___ Ask 'em my ques - tions and

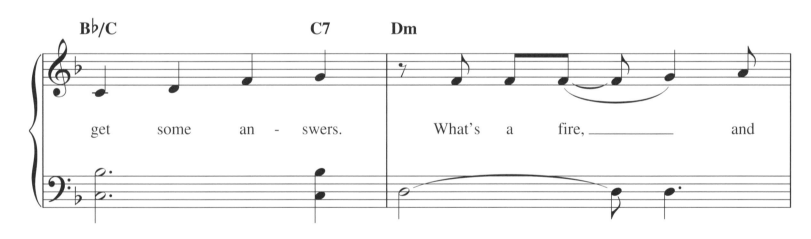

get some an - swers. What's a fire, _____ and

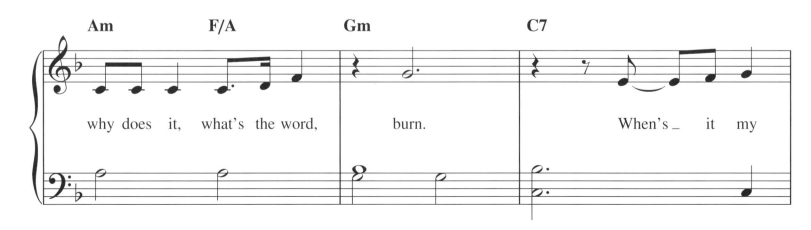

why does it, what's the word, burn. When's_ it my

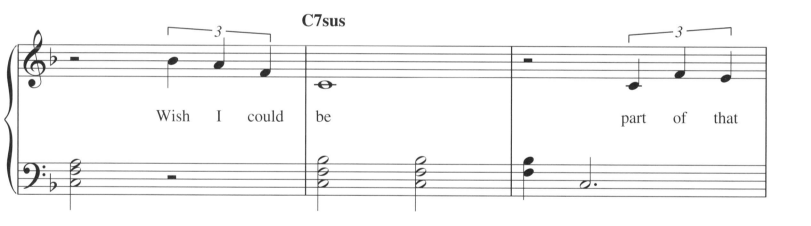

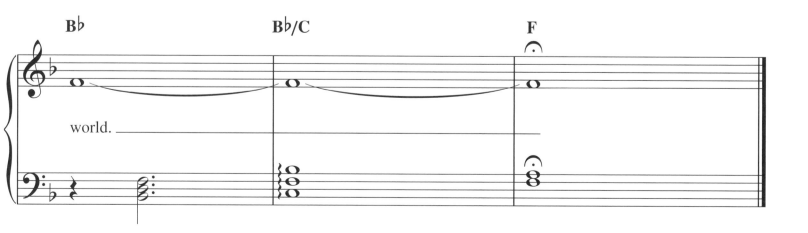

ONE JUMP AHEAD

from Walt Disney's ALADDIN

Music by ALAN MENKEN
Words by TIM RICE

Moderately

Aladdin: Got - ta keep   one jump a -

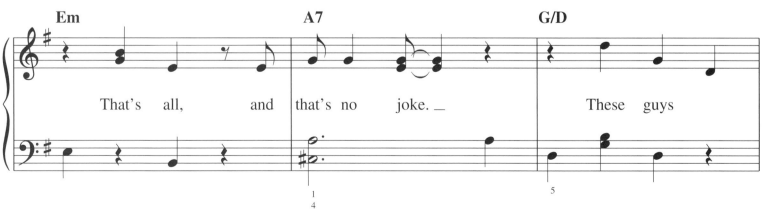

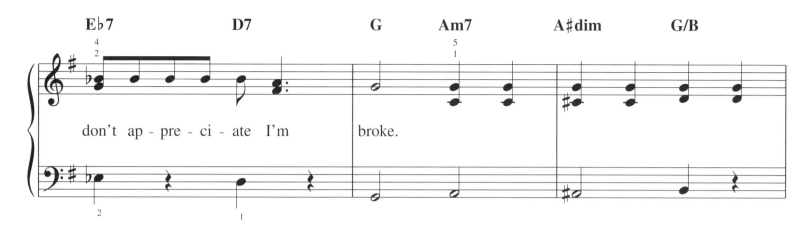

don't ap - pre - ci - ate I'm broke.

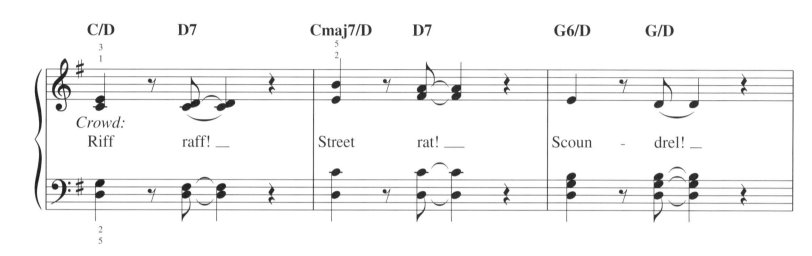

Crowd:
Riff raff! __ Street rat! __ Scoun - drel! __

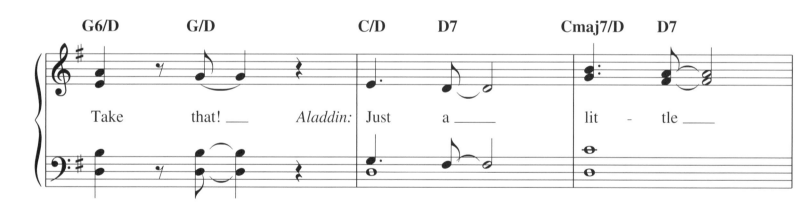

Take that! __ *Aladdin:* Just a _____ lit - tle _____

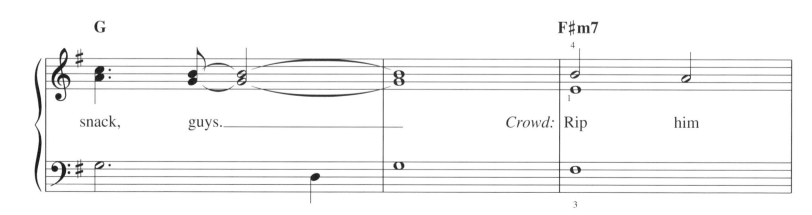

snack, guys._____ *Crowd:* Rip him

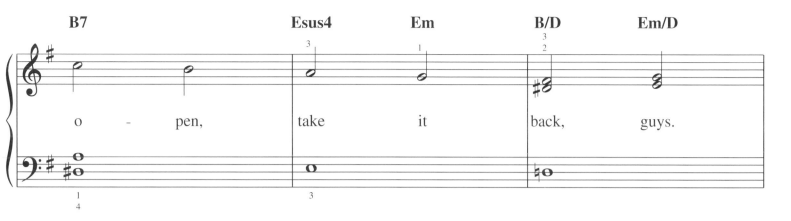

o - pen, take it back, guys.

Aladdin:
I can take a hint, got-ta face the facts. You're my on-ly friend, A -

bu! Who? *Ladies:* Oh, it's sad A - lad-din's hit the

bot - tom. He's be - come a

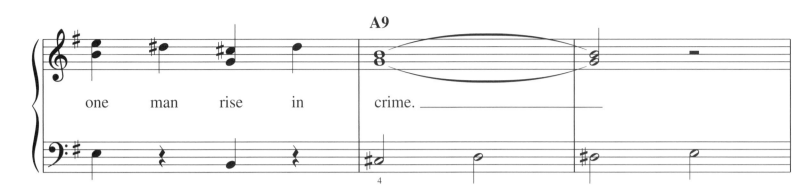

A9

one man rise in crime. _____

Dm

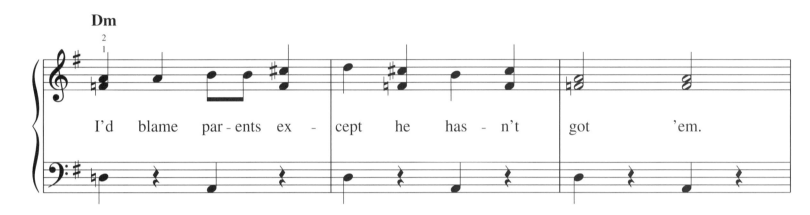

I'd blame par - ents ex - cept he has - n't got 'em.

F#7

Aladdin:
Got - ta eat to live, got - ta steal to eat, tell you all a -

B **B7** **Em**

bout it when I got the time! One jump a -

head of the slow - pokes.　　One skip a - head of my doom. ＿

Next time　　gon - na use a nom de　plume.

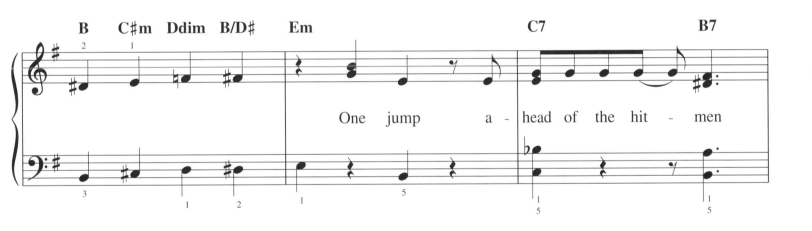

One jump a - head of the hit - men

one hit a - head of the flock. ＿　　I think I'll

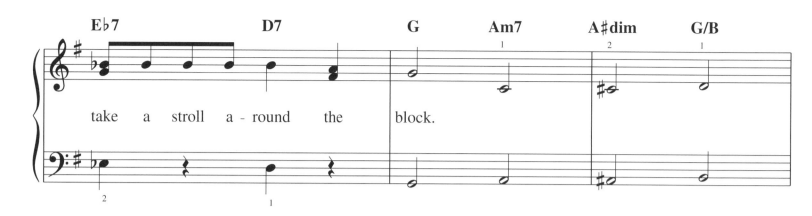

take a stroll a - round the block.

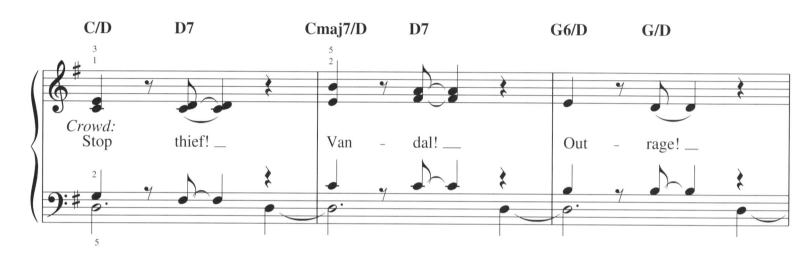

Crowd: Stop thief! __ Van - dal! __ Out - rage! __

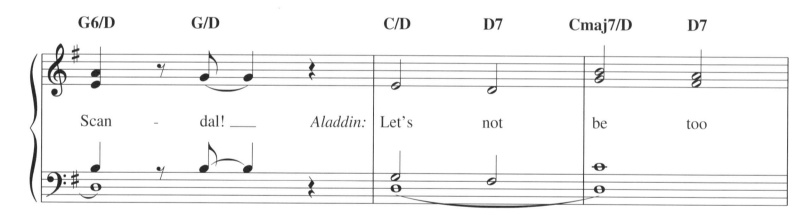

Scan - dal! ___ *Aladdin:* Let's not be too

hast - y. *Lady:* Still I

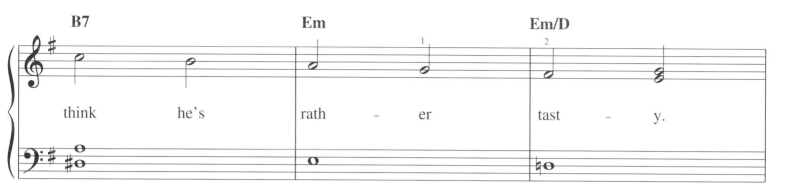

think   he's   rath – er   tast – y.

Aladdin:
Got – ta   eat   to   live,   got – ta   steal   to   eat,

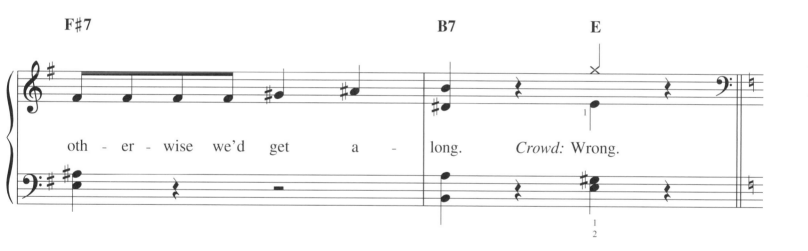

oth – er – wise   we'd   get   a –   long.   *Crowd:* Wrong.

Swing eighths

A(no 3rd)

Aladdin: One jump a - head of the hoof ___ beats.

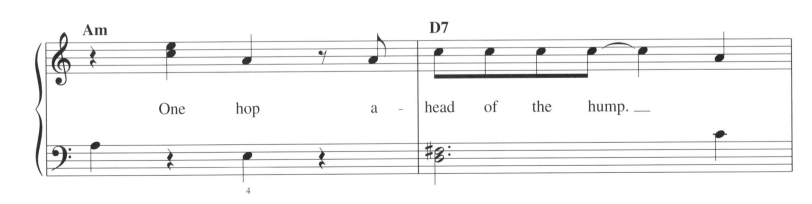

One hop a - head of the hump. ___

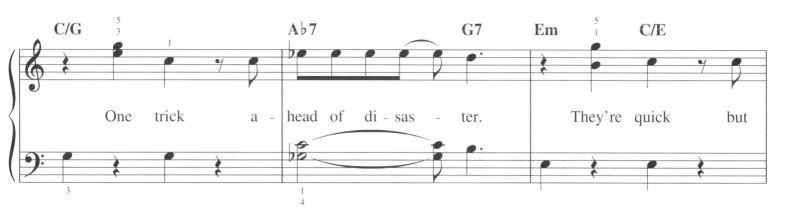

One trick a - head of di - sas - ter. They're quick but

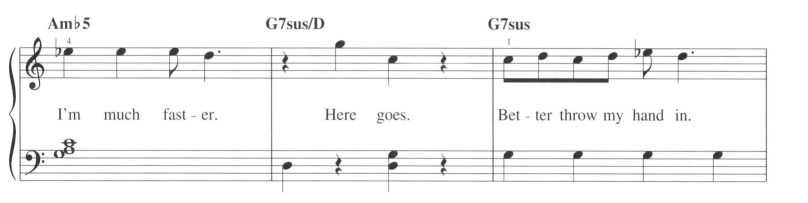

I'm much fast - er. Here goes. Bet - ter throw my hand in.

Wish me hap - py land-in'. All I got - ta do is jump!

OUR TOWN
from the Disney/Pixar film CARS

Words and Music by
RANDY NEWMAN

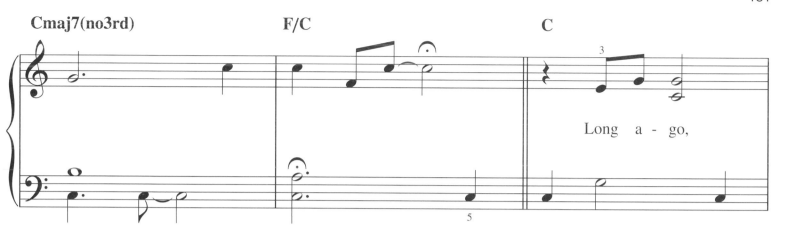

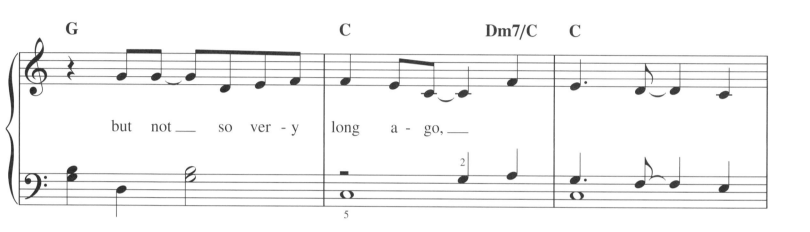

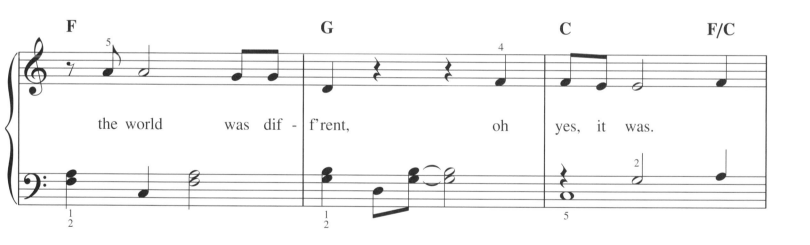

made it there ____ and you watched it grow. It was

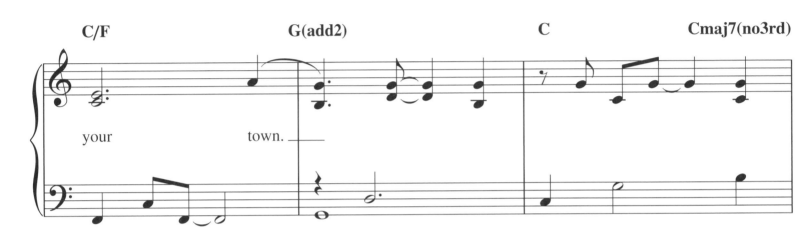

your town. ____

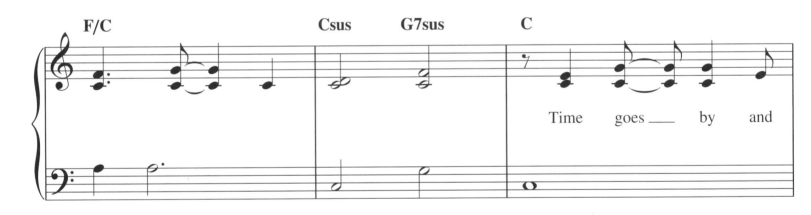

Time goes ____ by and

time brings chang - es, and you change too.

Noth - ing comes that you can't han - dle, so on you go. ____

You nev - er see it com - ing when the

world caves in on you, ____ on your town. ____

____ There's noth - ing you can do.

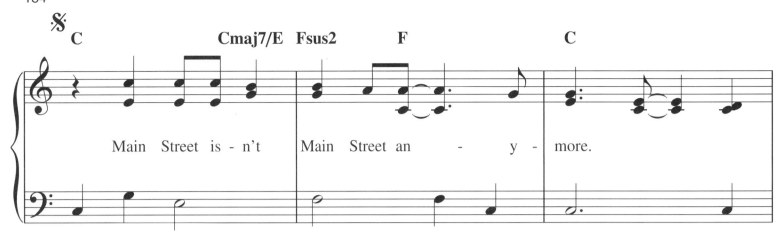

Main Street is-n't Main Street an - y - more.

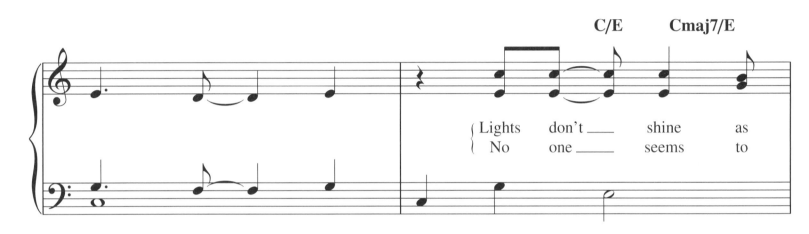

Lights don't ___ shine as
No one ___ seems to

bright - ly as they've shone be - fore. ___
meet us like they did be - fore. ___

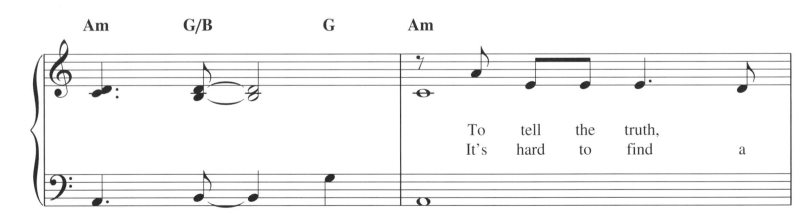

To tell the truth,
It's hard to find a

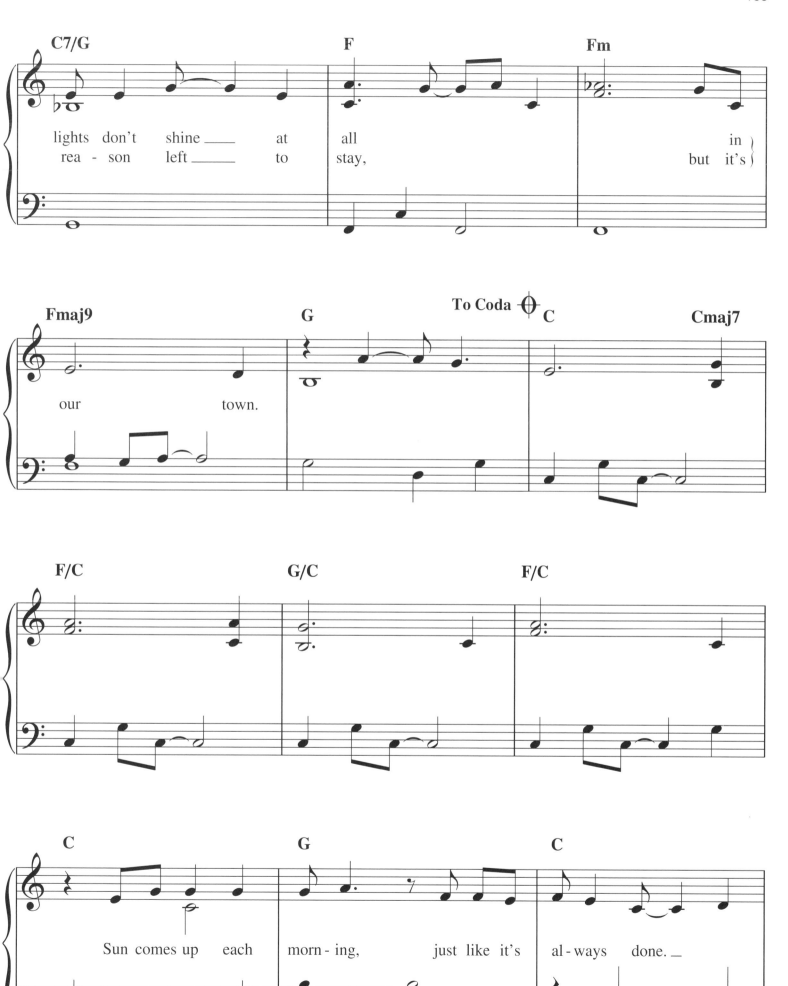

Get up and go to work and start the

day. _____ You o - pen up for

busi - ness; it's nev - er gon - na come as the

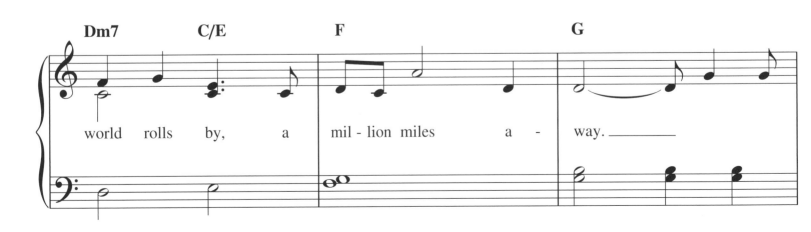

world rolls by, a mil - lion miles a - way. _____

REFLECTION
(Pop Version)
from Walt Disney Pictures' MULAN

Music by MATTHEW WILDER
Lyrics by DAVID ZIPPEL

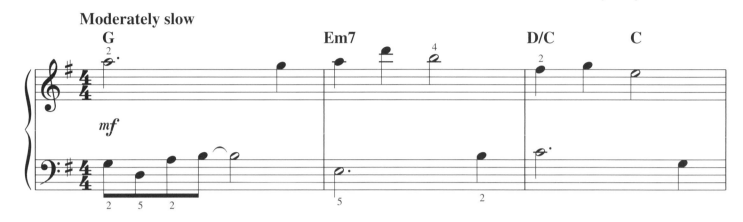

Look at me, you may think you see ___ who I

___ real - ly am, ___ but you'll nev - er know me. Ev - 'ry day it's

as if I play ___ a part. ___

Now I see if I
but some-how I will

Gm7   **Cm7**   **E♭m6**

wear a mask   I can   fool   the world,   but I can - not fool   my ___
show the world   what's in - side   my heart   and be loved for who   I ___

B♭   **%**

heart.   Who   is that
am.   Who   is that
      Why   must we

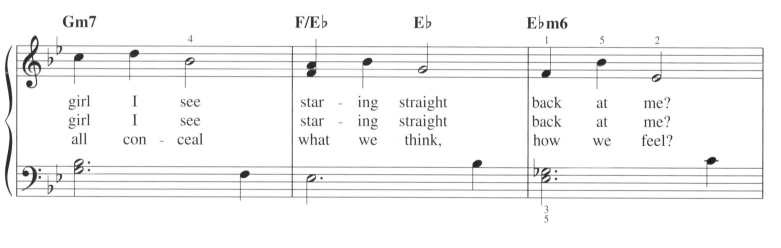

Gm7   **F/E♭**   **E♭**   **E♭m6**

girl I see   star - ing straight   back at me?
girl I see   star - ing straight   back at me?
all con - ceal   what we think,   how we feel?

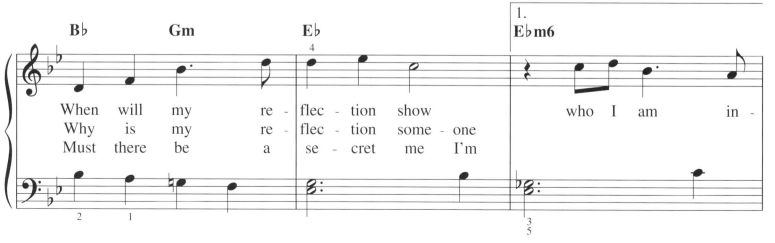

B♭   **Gm**   **E♭**   **1.** **E♭m6**

When will my re - flec - tion show   who I am in -
Why is my re - flec - tion some - one
Must there be a se - cret me I'm

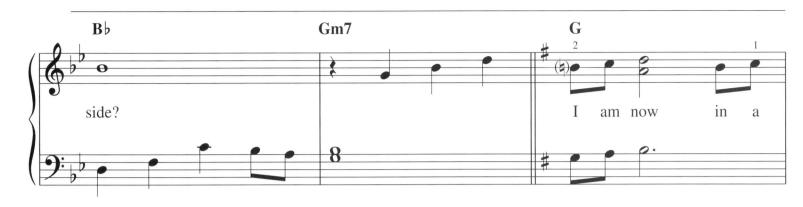

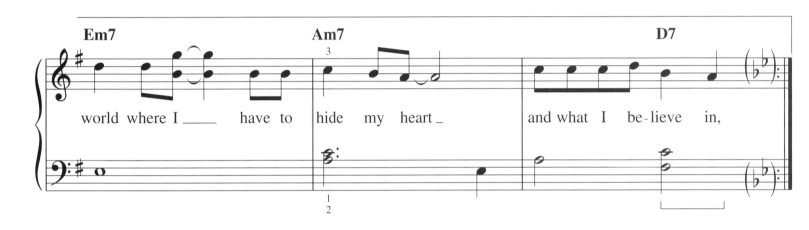

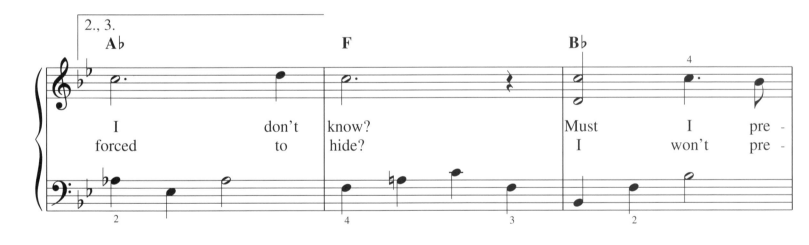

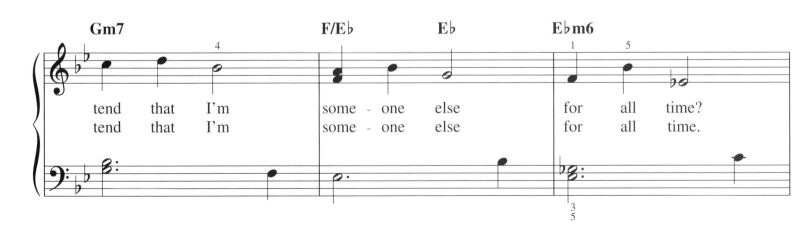

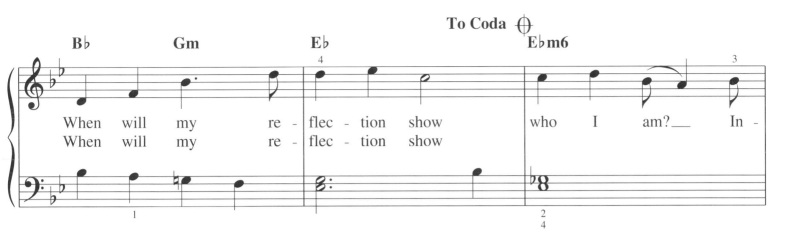

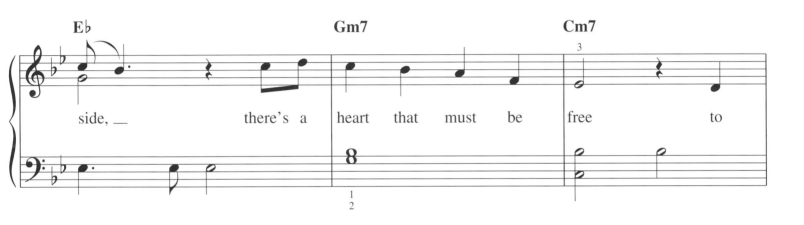

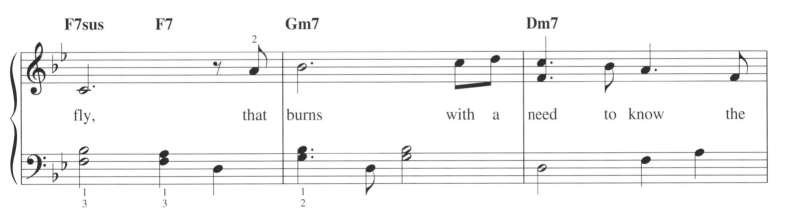

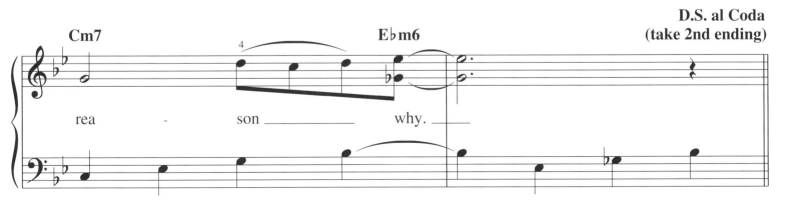

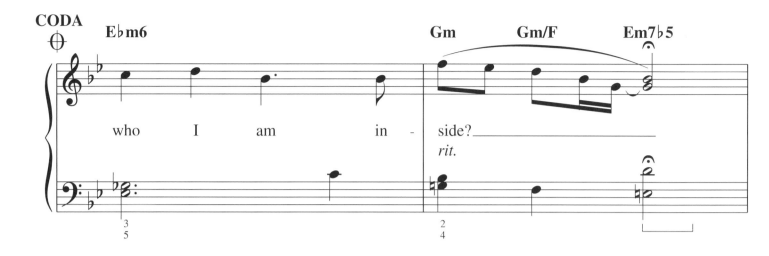

CODA

Ebm6   Gm   Gm/F   Em7b5

who I am in - side? _____
rit.

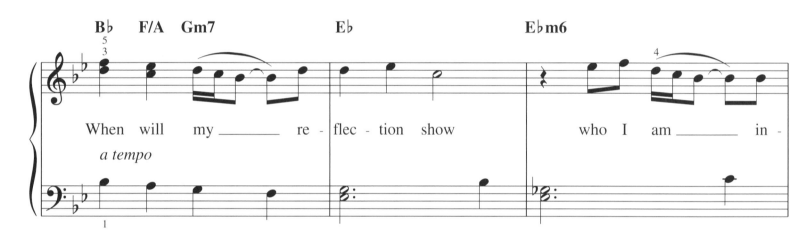

Bb   F/A   Gm7   Eb   Ebm6

When will my _____ re - flec - tion show   who I am _____ in -
a tempo

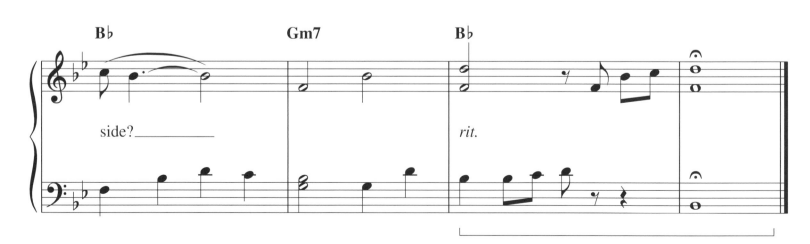

Bb   Gm7   Bb

side? _____   *rit.*

TWO WORLDS

from Walt Disney Pictures' TARZAN™

Words and Music by
PHIL COLLINS

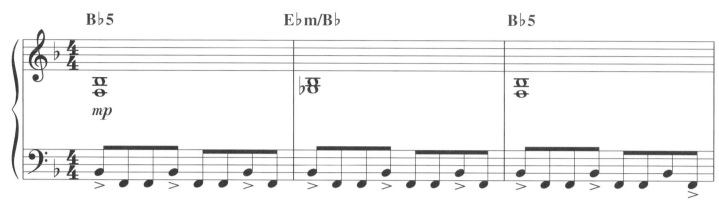

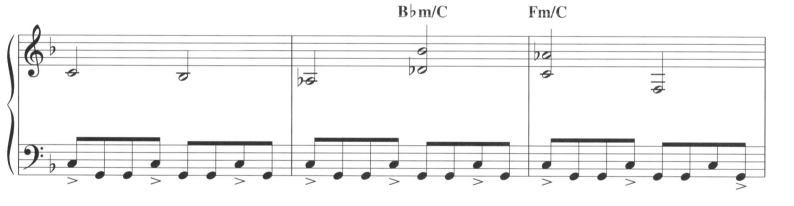

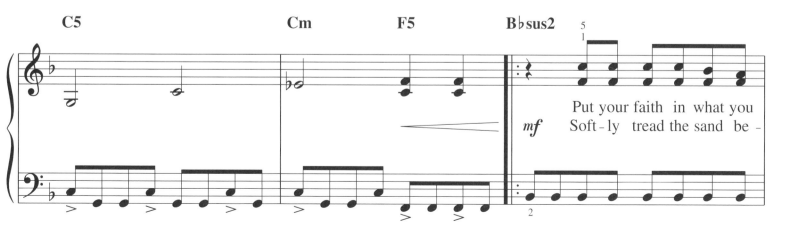

Put your faith in what you
Soft-ly tread the sand be -

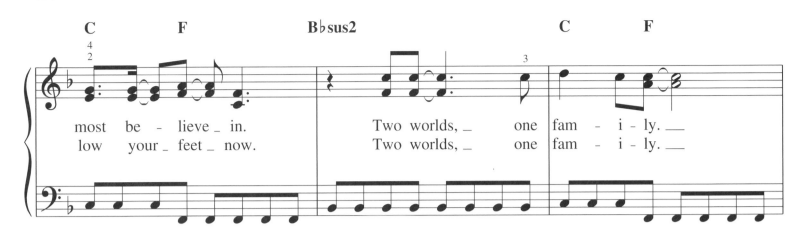

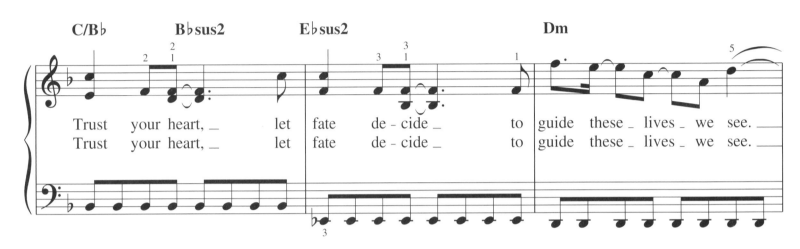

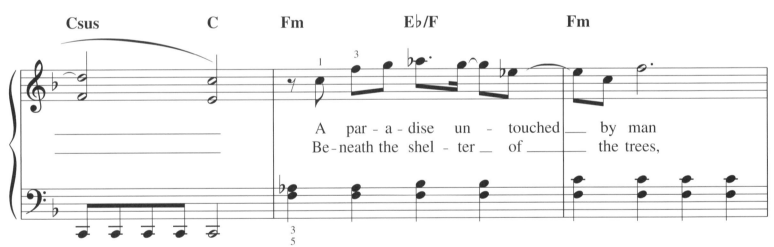

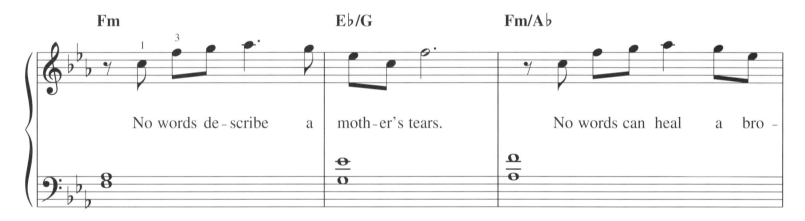

No words de-scribe a moth-er's tears. No words can heal a bro-

ken heart. A dream is gone;___ but where there's hope,

SOMEDAY
from Walt Disney's THE HUNCHBACK OF NOTRE DAME

Music by ALAN MENKEN
Lyrics by STEPHEN SCHWARTZ

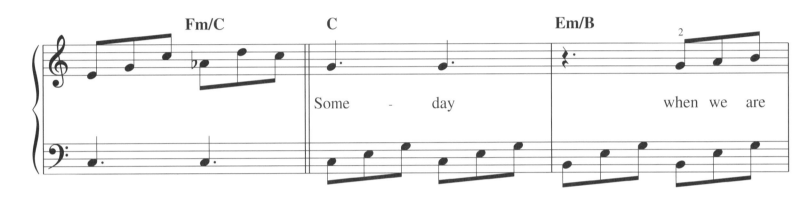

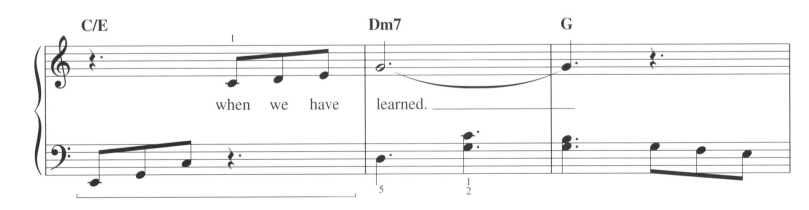

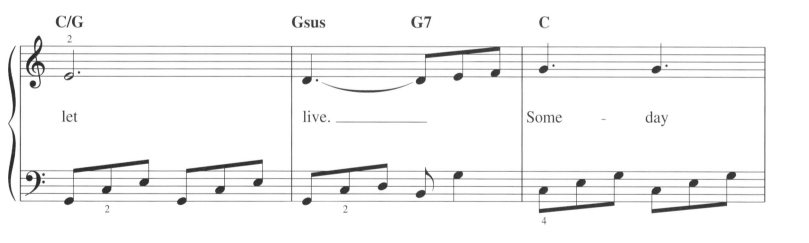

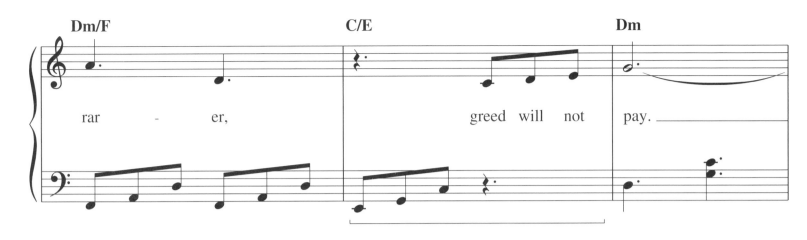

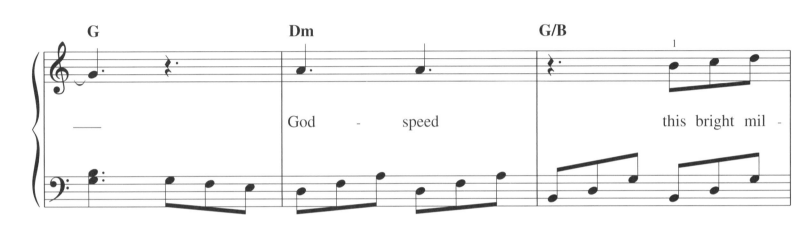

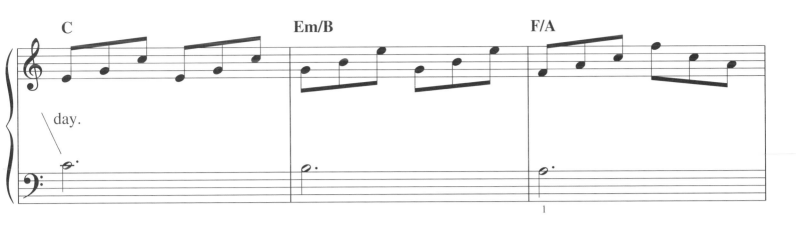

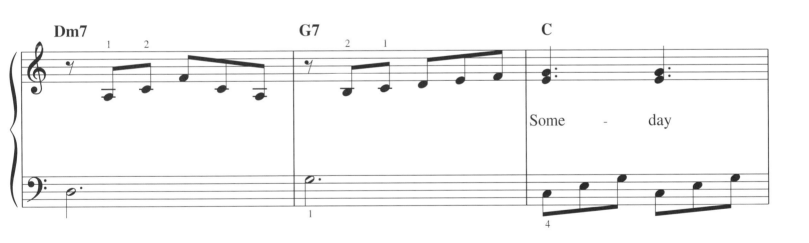

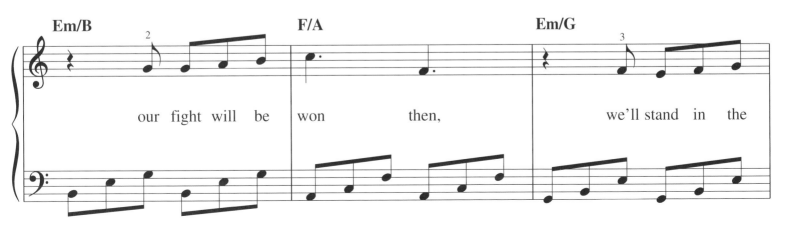

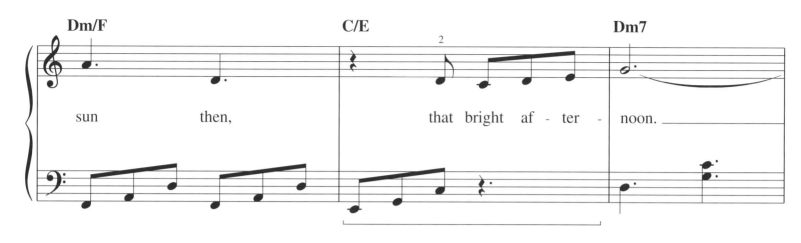

sun then, that bright af - ter - noon. _____

____ Till then, on days when the

sun is gone, we'll hang

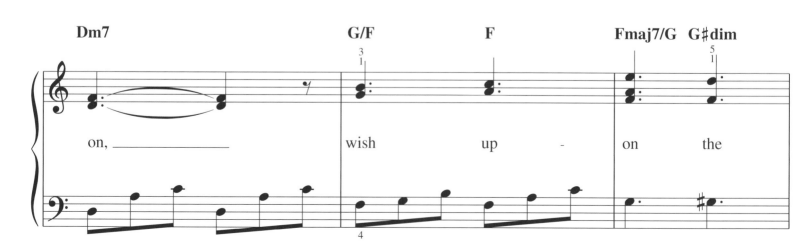

on, _____ wish up - on the

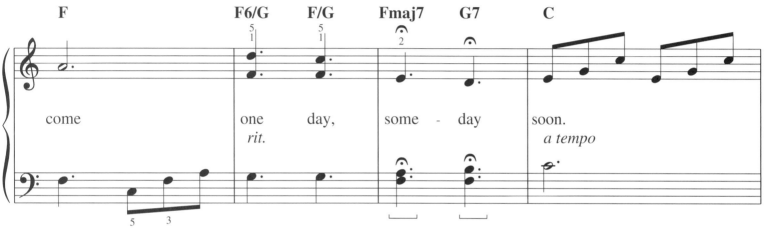

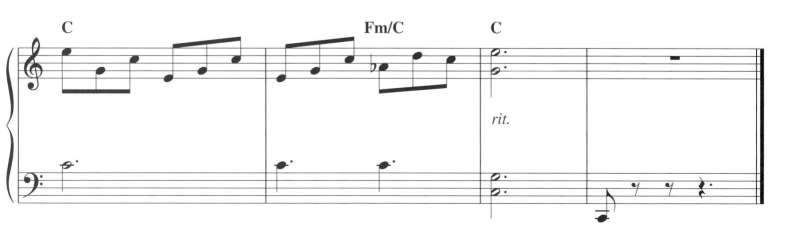

THAT'S HOW YOU KNOW

from Walt Disney Pictures' ENCHANTED

Music by ALAN MENKEN
Lyrics by STEPHEN SCHWARTZ

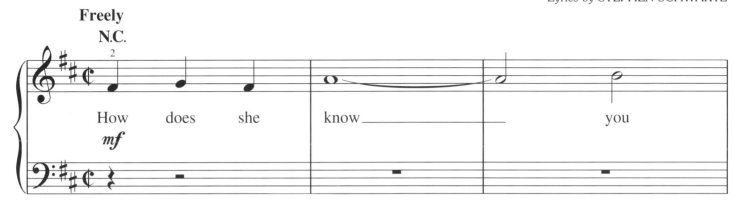

How does she know _____ you

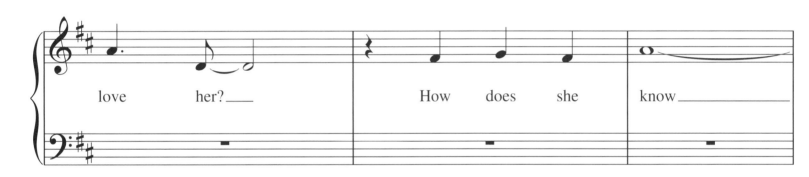

love her? ____ How does she know _____

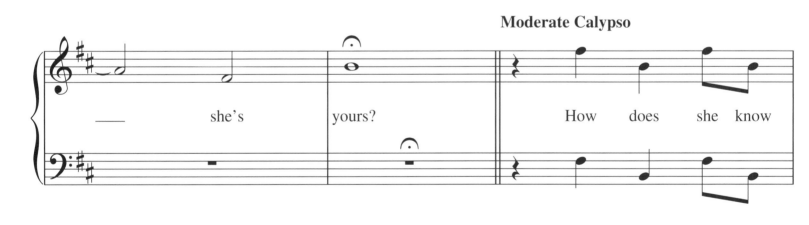

____ she's yours? How does she know

How does she know that you love her? How do you show

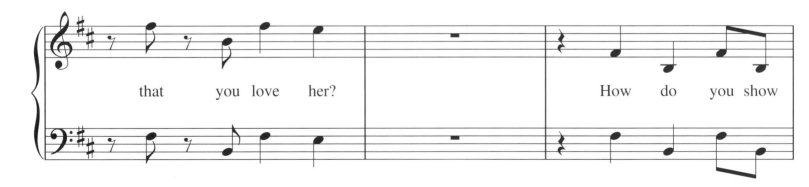

that you love her? How do you show

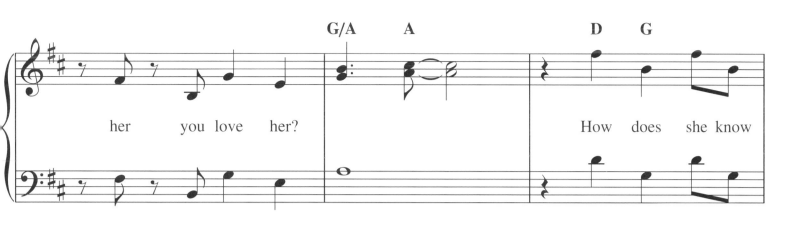

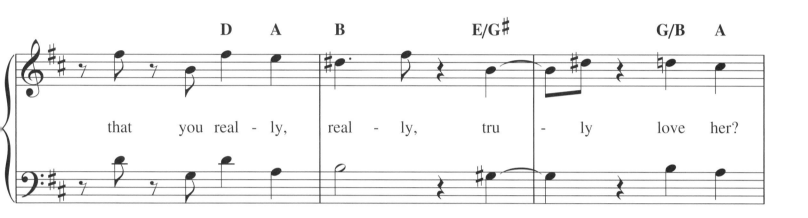

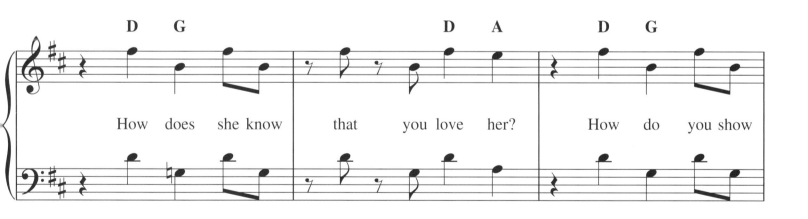

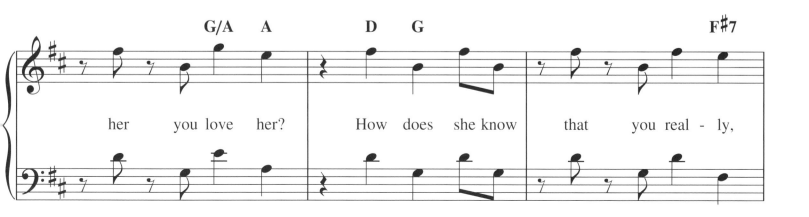

B   E   G   A   D

real - ly,   tru - ly   love her?   It's not   e - nough to take
Ev -'ry - bod - y wants   to live

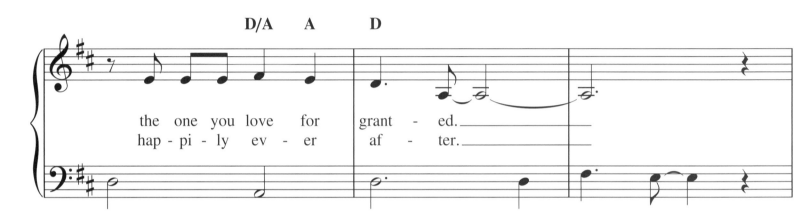

D/A   A   D

the one you love   for   grant - ed._____
hap - pi - ly   ev - er   af - ter._____

A   F#   B

You must   re - mind her, or_____ she'll be in-clined to   say:_____
Ev -'ry - bod - y wants to know_____ their true__ love is   true._____

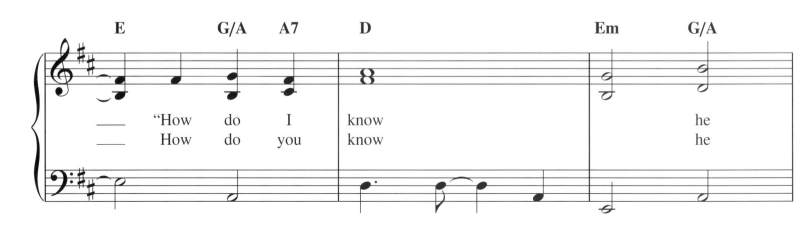

E   G/A   A7   D   Em   G/A

____ "How   do   I   know   he
____ How   do   you   know   he

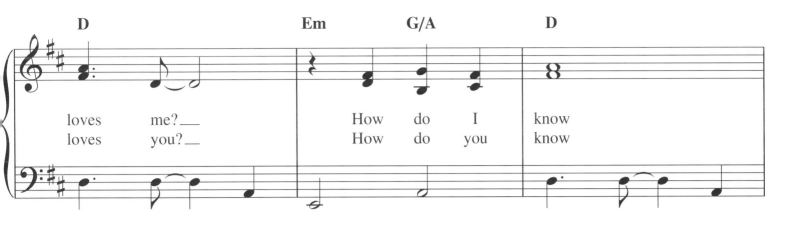

loves me?___
loves you?___
How do I know
How do you know

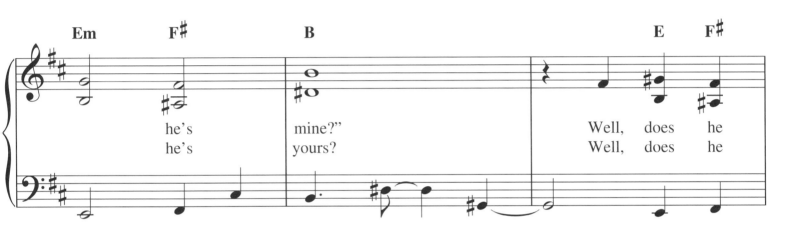

he's
he's
mine?"
yours?
Well, does he
Well, does he

leave a lit-tle note to
take you out___ danc-ing
tell you you are
just so he can
on
hold
his
you
mind?_
close?_

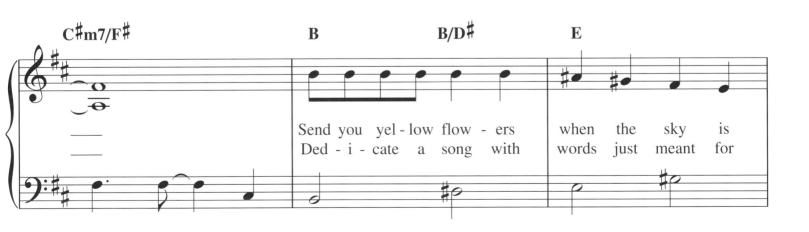

Send you yel-low flow-ers
Ded-i-cate a song with
when the sky is
words just meant for

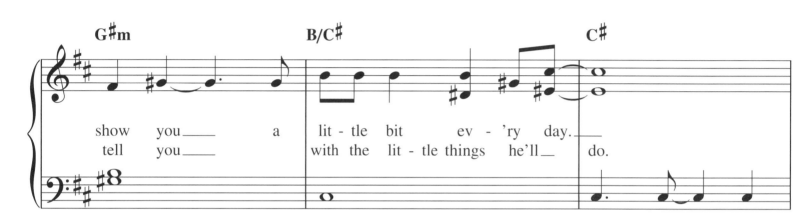

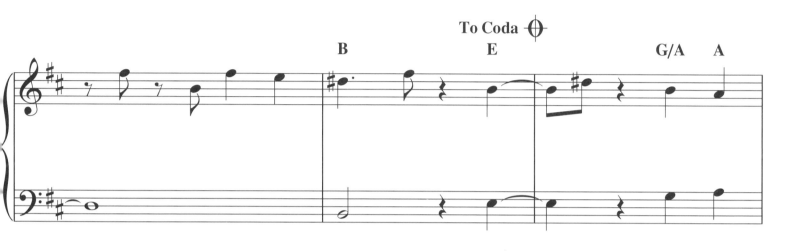

You've got to show her you need her; don't treat her like

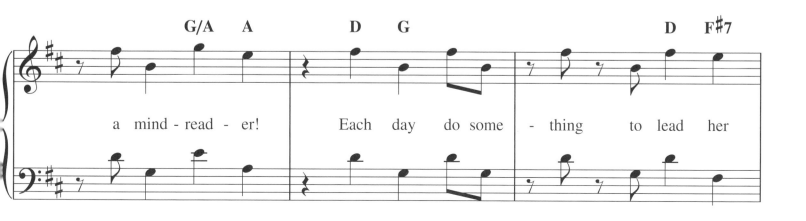

a mind - read - er! Each day do some - thing to lead her

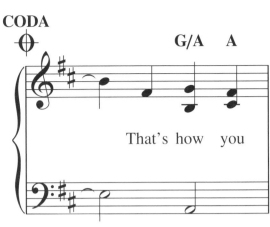

D.S. al Coda

CODA

B   E   G/A   A

G/A   A

to be - lieve ___ you love her.

That's how you

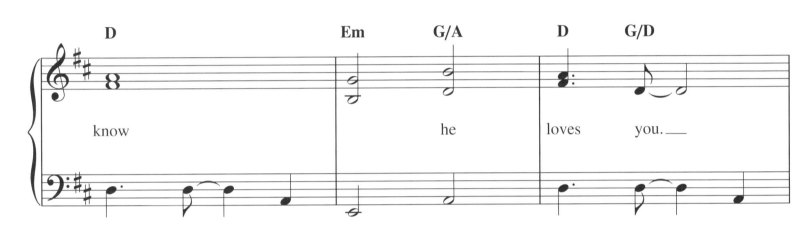

D   Em   G/A   D   G/D

know   he   loves you. ___

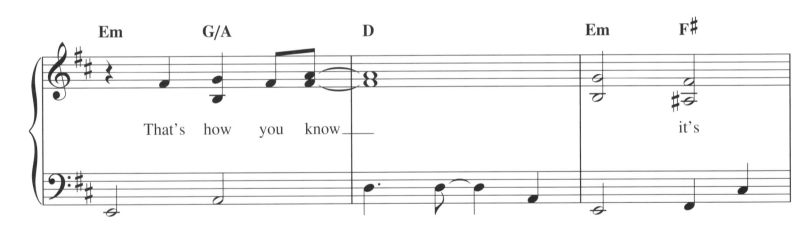

Em   G/A   D   Em   F#

That's how you know ___   it's

B   E   F#   B   B/D#

true.   Be - cause he'll   wear your fav-'rite col - or

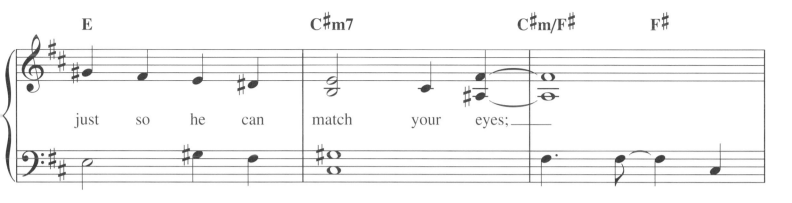

just so he can match your eyes;

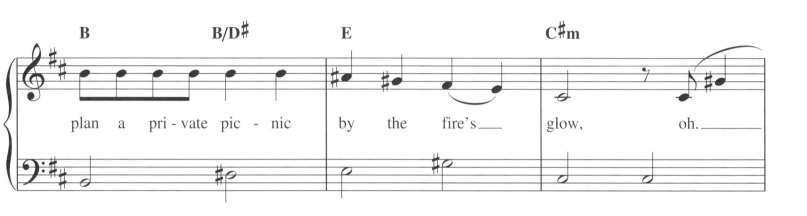

plan a pri - vate pic - nic by the fire's glow, oh.

His heart - 'll be yours for - ev - er,

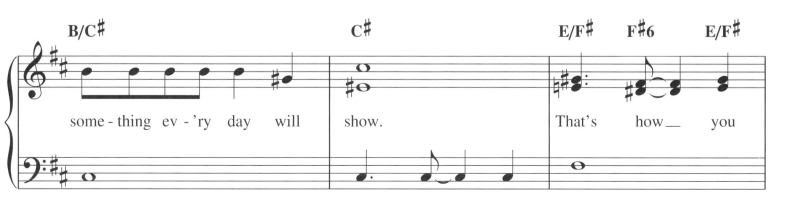

some - thing ev - 'ry day will show. That's how you

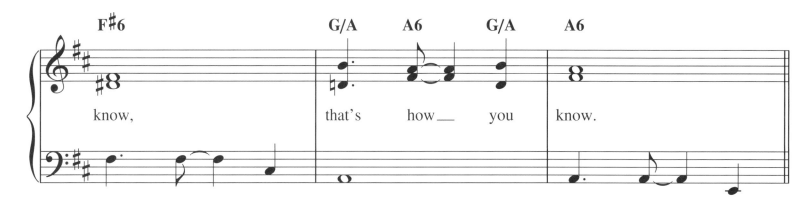

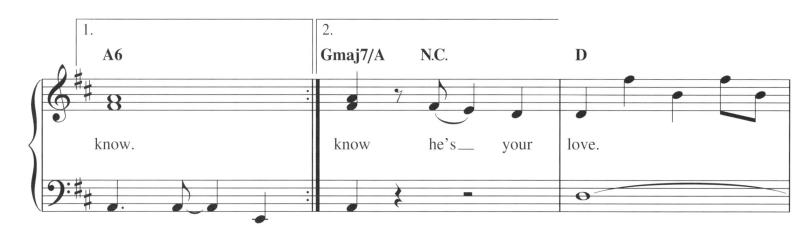

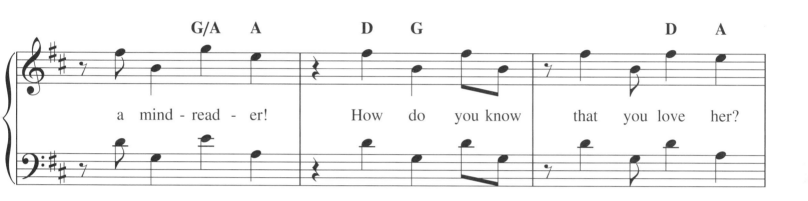

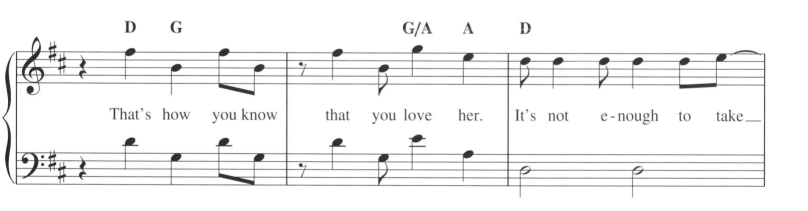

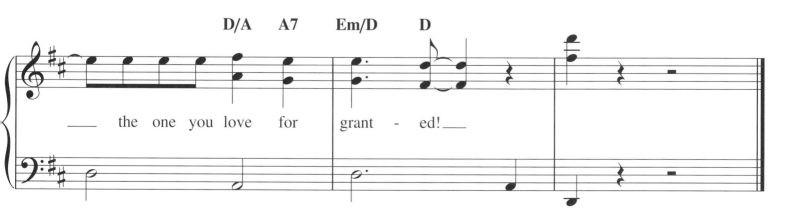

TRUE LOVE'S KISS
from Walt Disney Pictures' ENCHANTED

Music by ALAN MENKEN
Lyrics by STEPHEN SCHWARTZ

Easily, with freedom

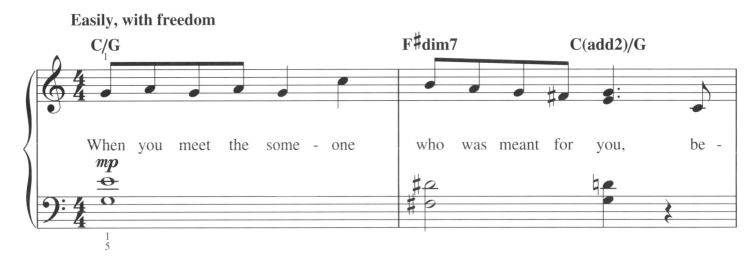

When you meet the some - one who was meant for you, be -

fore two can be - come one, there's some-thing you must do.

There is some-thing sweet-er

More flowing, still freely

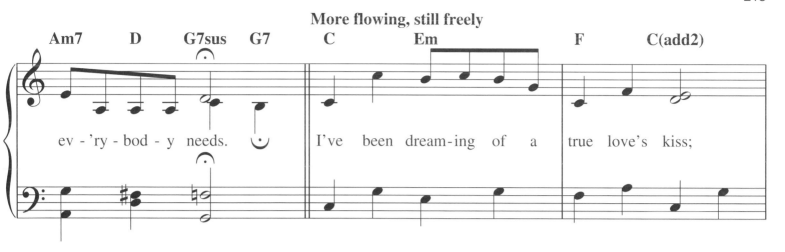

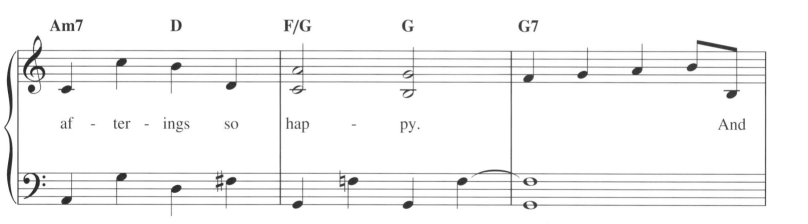

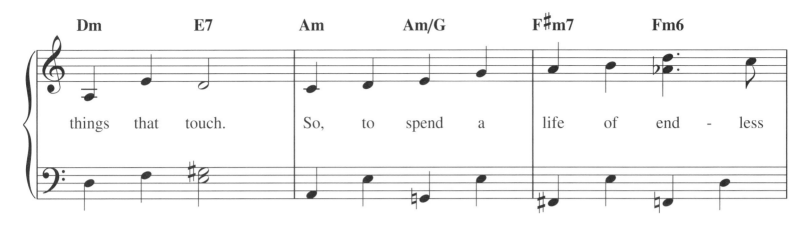

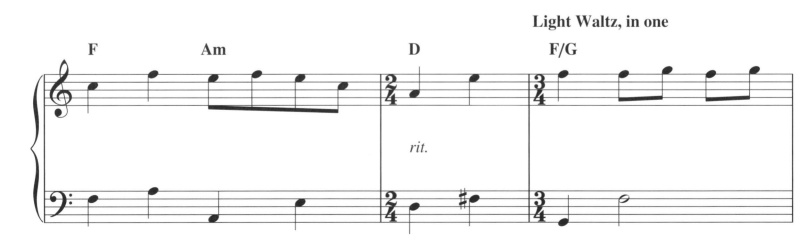

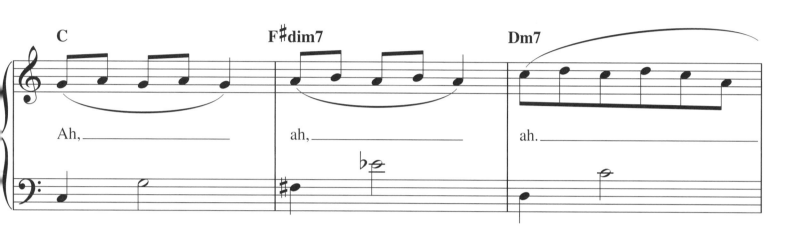

Ah,_____ ah,_____ ah._____

Ah,_____ ah,_____

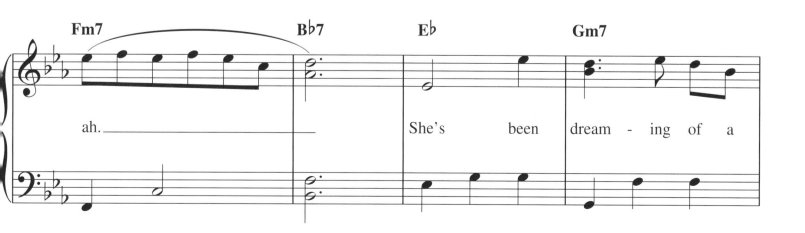

ah._____ She's been dream - ing of a

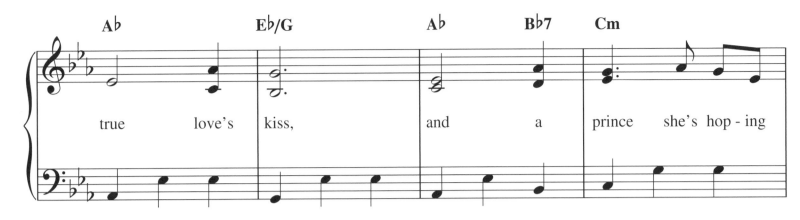

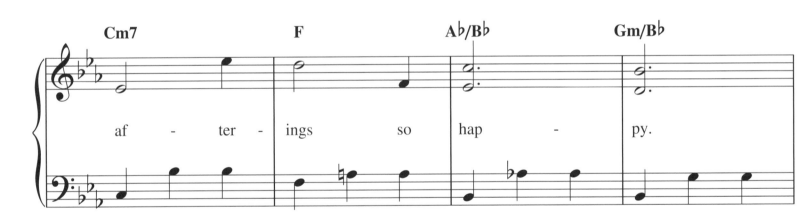

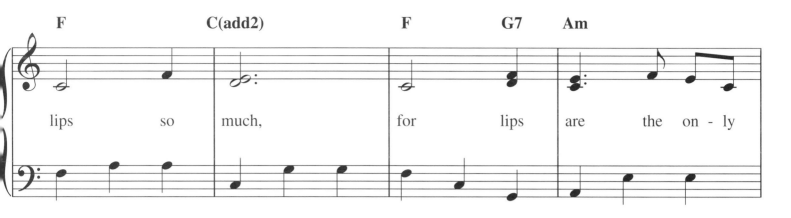

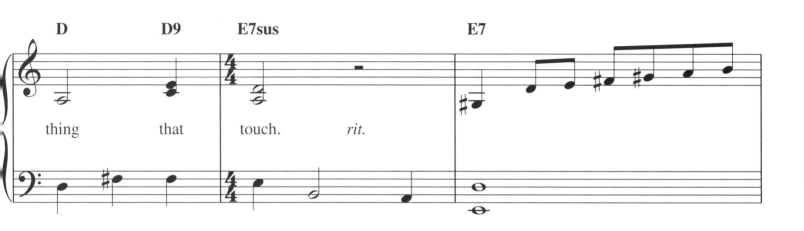

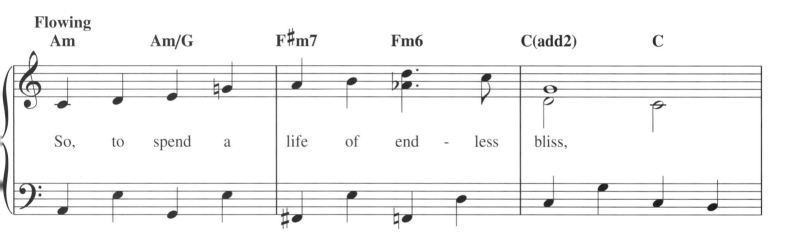

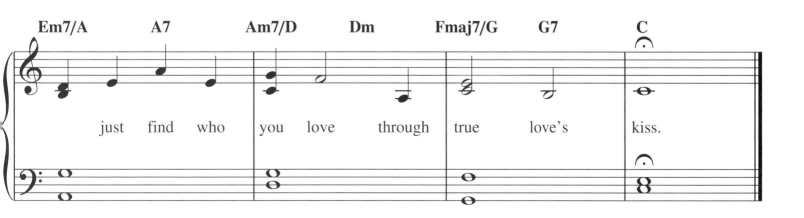

UNDER THE SEA
from Walt Disney's THE LITTLE MERMAID

Music by ALAN MENKEN
Lyrics by HOWARD ASHMAN

The sea - weed is al - ways green - er
Down here _ all the fish is hap - py

in some - bod - y el - se's lake.
as off _ through the waves dey roll.

You dream _ a - bout
The fish _ on the

go - ing up there.
land ain't hap - py.

But that _ is a
They sad _ 'cause they

big mis - take.
in the bowl.

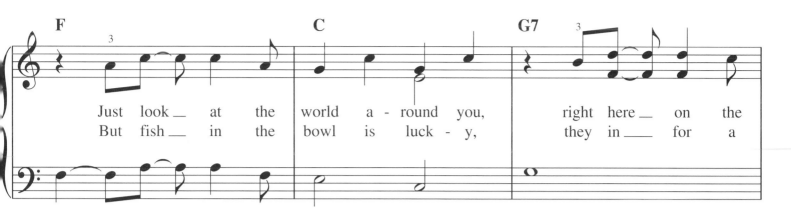

Just look __ at the world a - round you,
But fish __ in the bowl is luck - y,

right here __ on the
they in __ for a

o - cean floor.
wors - er fate.

Such won - der - ful
One day __ when the

things sur - round you.
boss get hun - gry

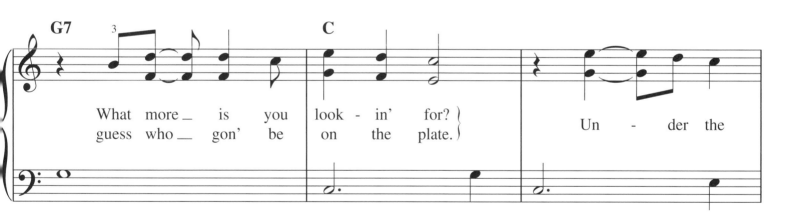

What more __ is you
guess who __ gon' be

look - in' for?
on the plate.

Un - der the

sea,

un - der the sea.

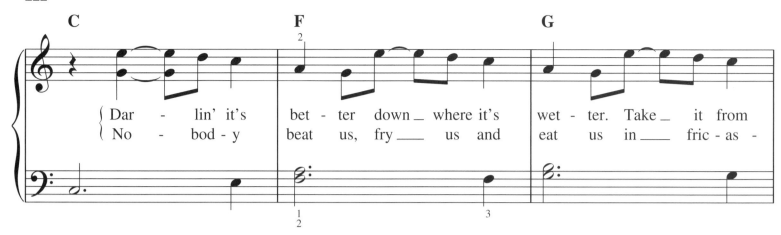

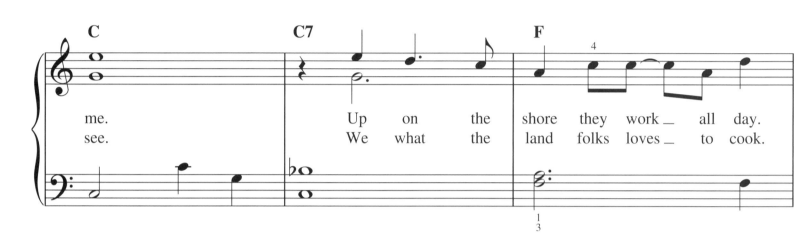

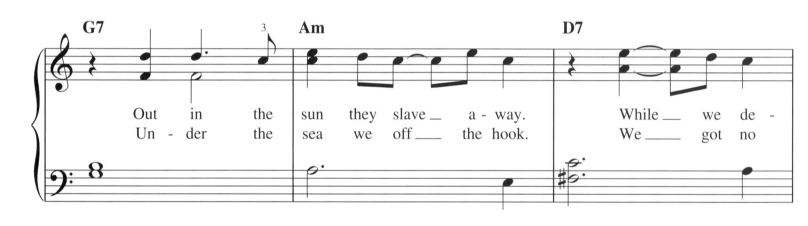

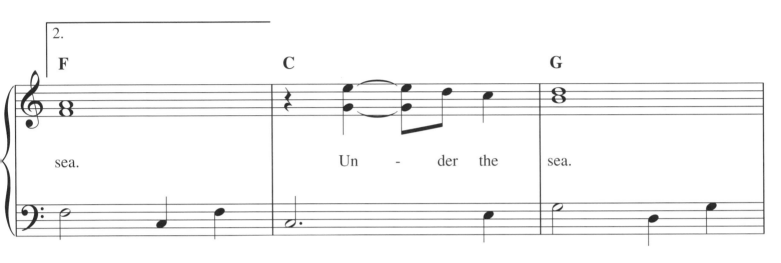

sea. Un - der the sea.

Since life is sweet here we ___ got the beat here nat - u - ral -

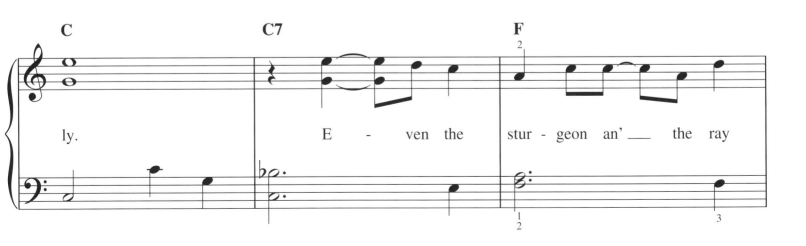

ly. E - ven the stur - geon an' ___ the ray

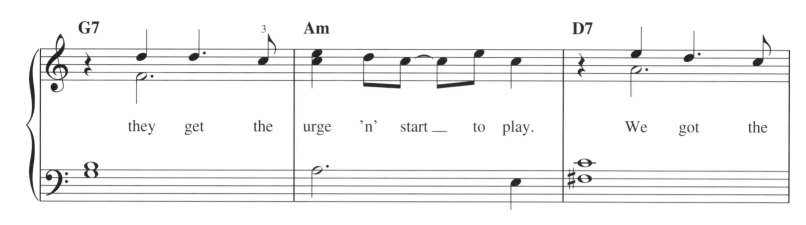

they get the urge 'n' start __ to play. We got the

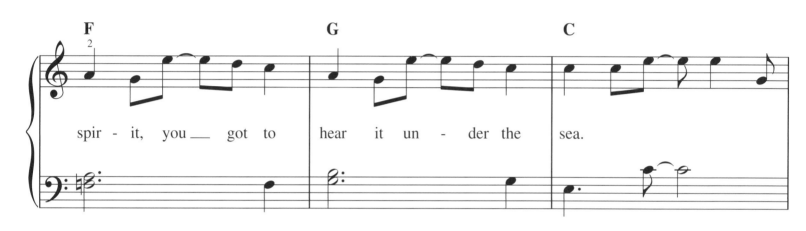

spir - it, you __ got to hear it un - der the sea.

The newt play the flute. The carp play the harp. The

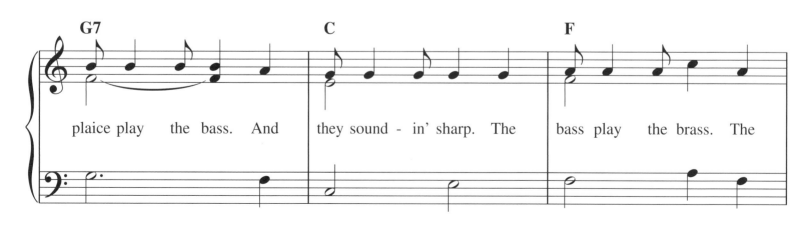

plaice play the bass. And they sound - in' sharp. The bass play the brass. The

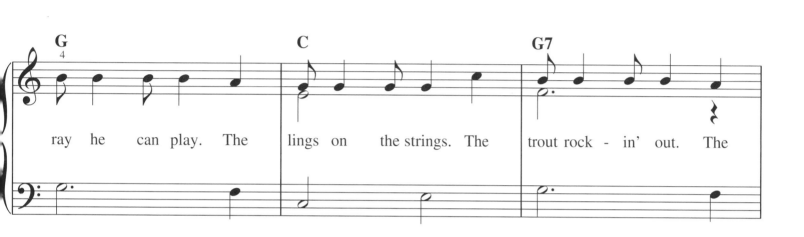

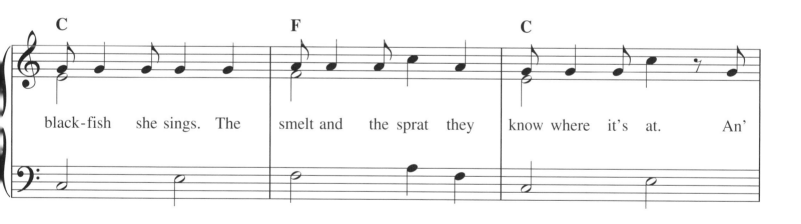

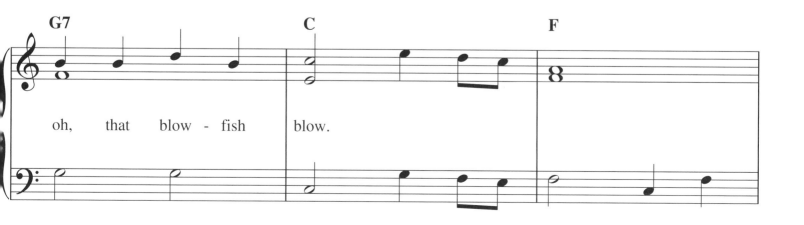

Un-der the sea. Un-der the

sea. When the sar - dine be - gin ___ the be - guine it's mu - sic to

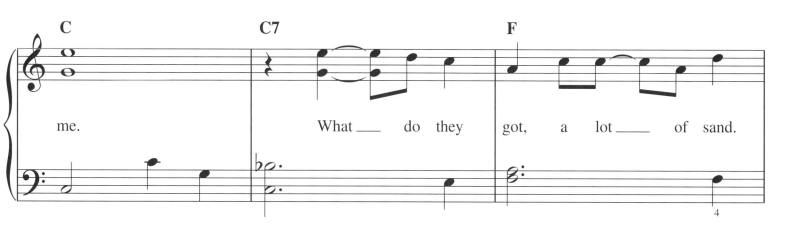

me. What ___ do they got, a lot ___ of sand.

We got a hot crus - ta - ce - an band. Each ___ lit - tle

clam here know_ how to | jam here un - der the | sea. | Each lit-tle
slug here cut - tin' a | rug here un - der the | sea. | Each lit-tle

snail here know_ how to | wail here. That's_ why it's | hot-ter un - der the

wa - ter. Ya_ we in | luck here down_ in the | muck here un - der the

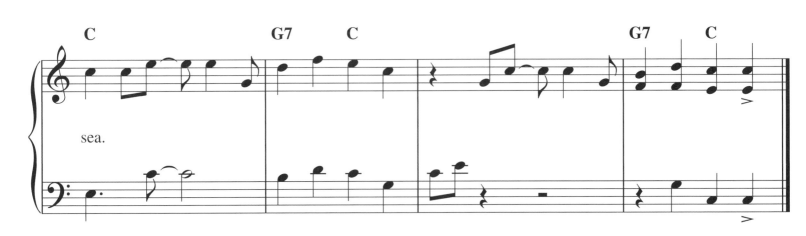

sea.

WHAT I'VE BEEN LOOKING FOR

from the Disney Channel Original Movie HIGH SCHOOL MUSICAL

Words and Music by ANDY DODD
and ADAM WATTS

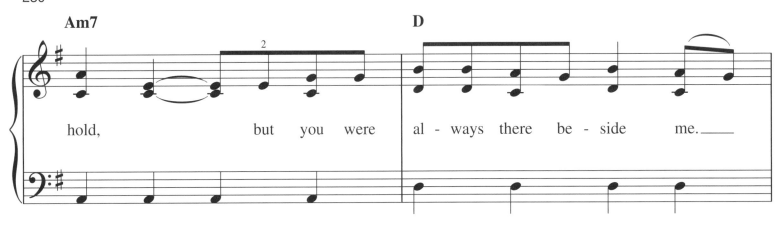

hold, but you were al - ways there be - side me.____

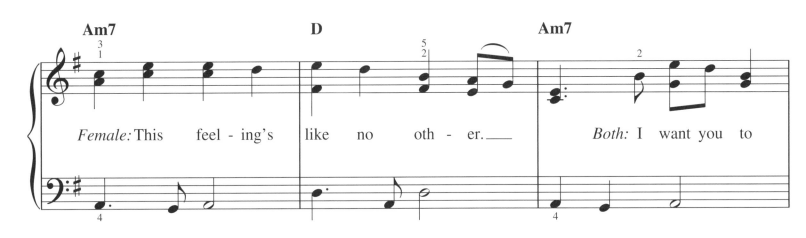

Female: This feel - ing's like no oth - er.____ *Both:* I want you to

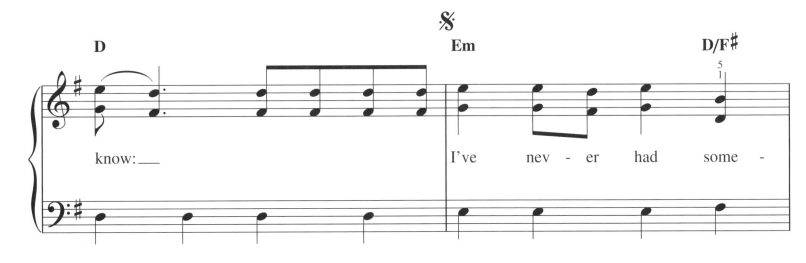

know:____ I've nev - er had some -

one who knows me like you do,____ the way you

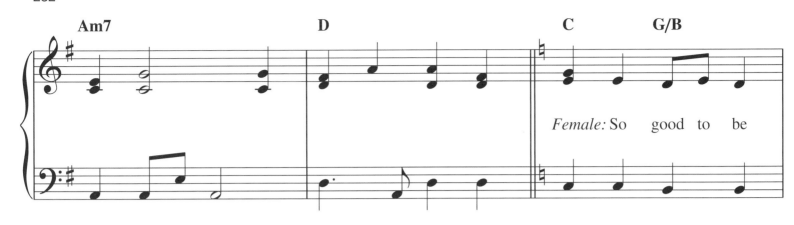

WE'RE ALL IN THIS TOGETHER

from the Disney Channel Original Movie HIGH SCHOOL MUSICAL

Words and Music by MATTHEW GERRARD
and ROBBIE NEVIL

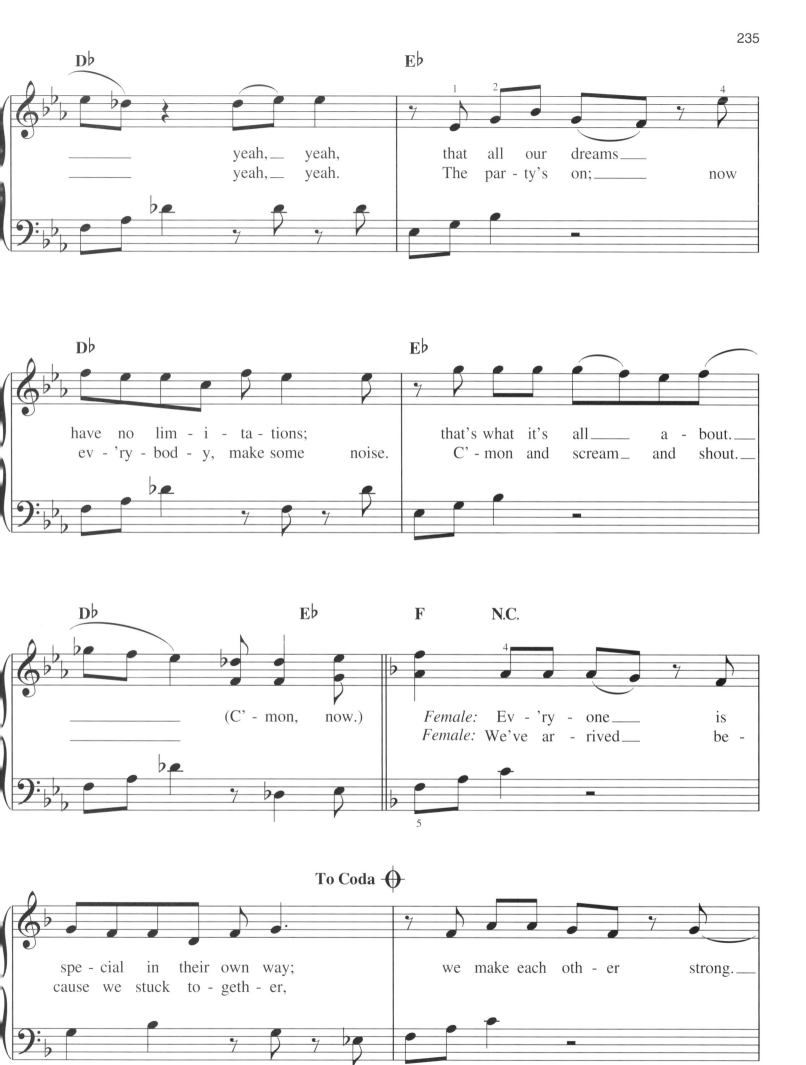

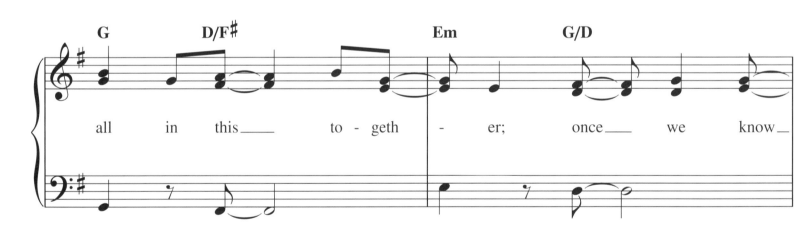

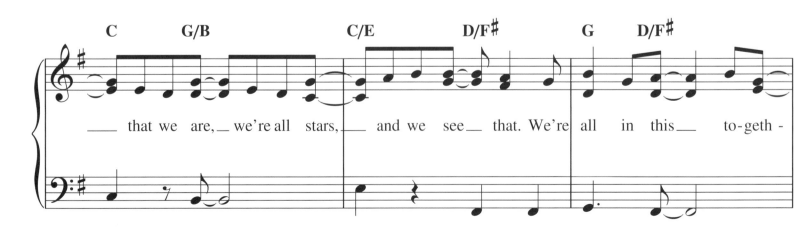

- er, and__ it shows__ when we stand__ hand in hand,__ __ make our dreams__ come__ true.__ Ev-'ry-bod-y now:

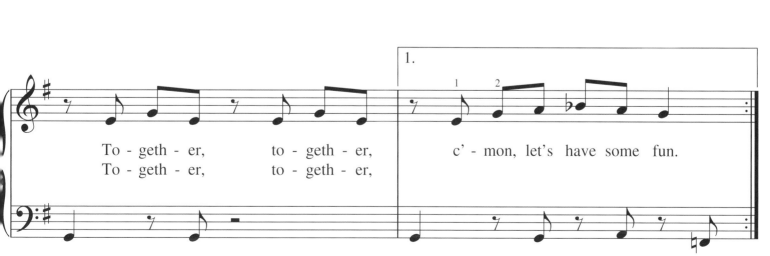

To-geth-er, to-geth-er, to-geth-er, ev-'ry-one.
To-geth-er, we're there for each oth-er ev-'ry time.

To-geth-er, to-geth-er, c'-mon, let's have some fun.
To-geth-er, to-geth-er,

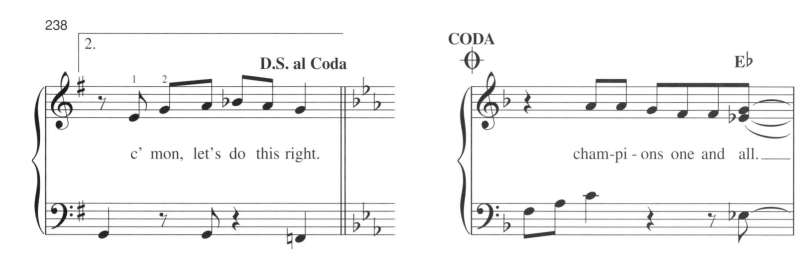

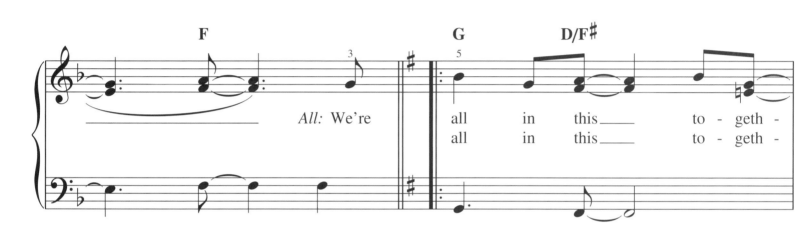

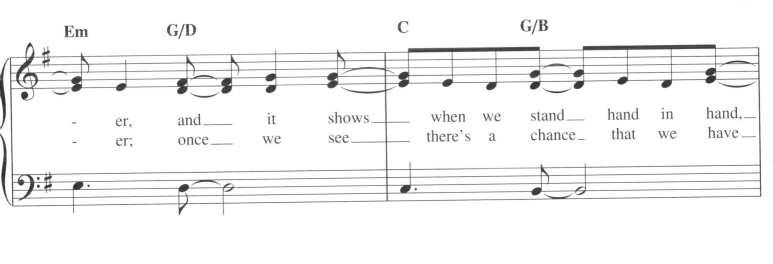

WHEN SHE LOVED ME
from Walt Disney Pictures' TOY STORY 2 - A Pixar Film

Music and Lyrics by
RANDY NEWMAN

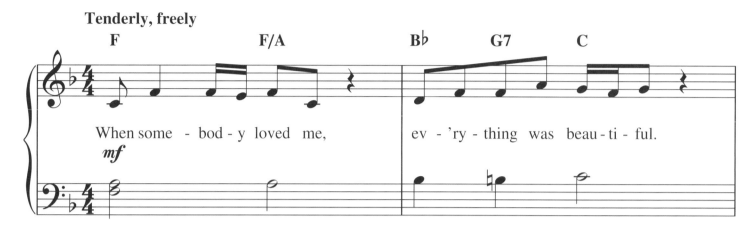

When some - bod - y loved me, ev - 'ry - thing was beau - ti - ful.

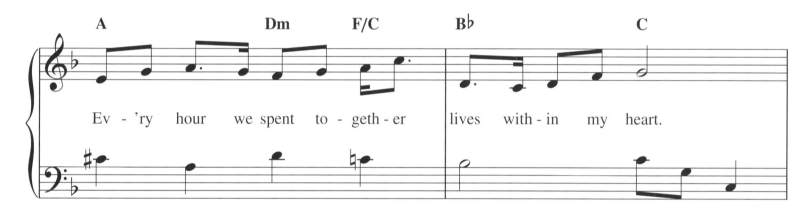

Ev - 'ry hour we spent to - geth - er lives with - in my heart.

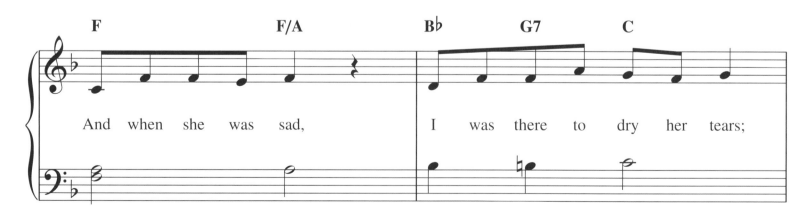

And when she was sad, I was there to dry her tears;

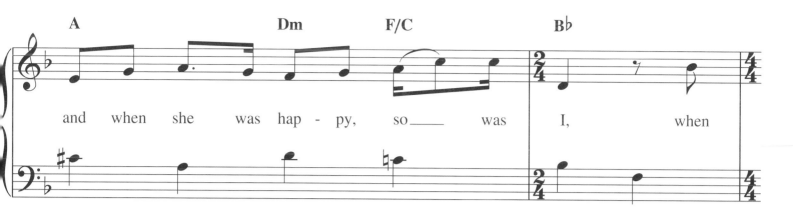

and when she was hap - py, so___ was I, when

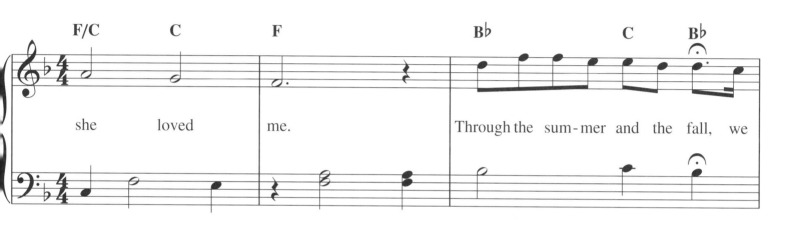

she loved me. Through the sum-mer and the fall, we

had each oth - er, that was all. Just she and I to - geth - er, like

it was meant to be. And when she was lone - ly,

I was there to com - fort her, and I know_____ that

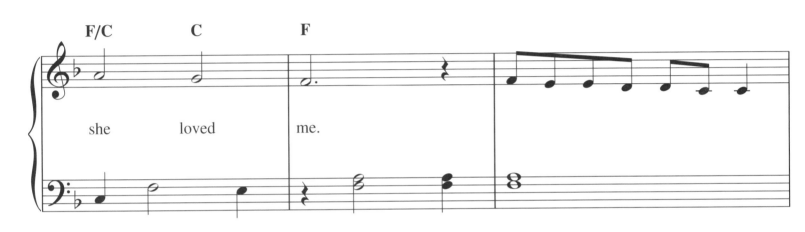

she loved me.

So the years went by; I stayed the same. But

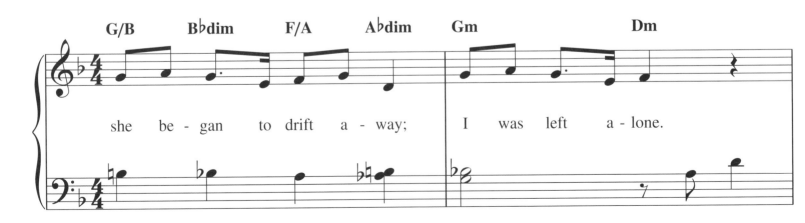

she be - gan to drift a - way; I was left a - lone.

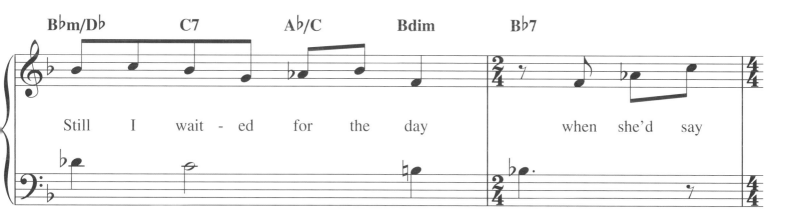

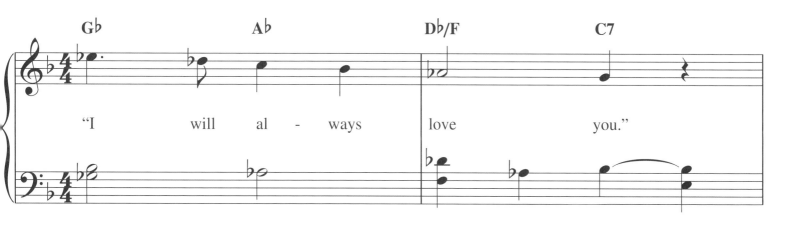

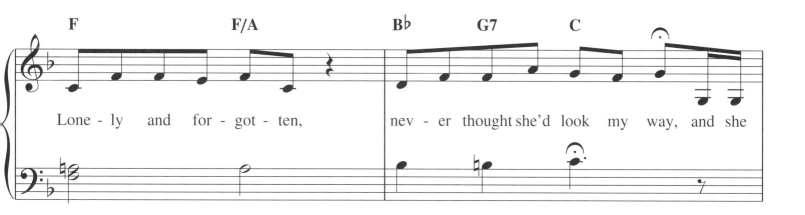

loved me when she loved me.

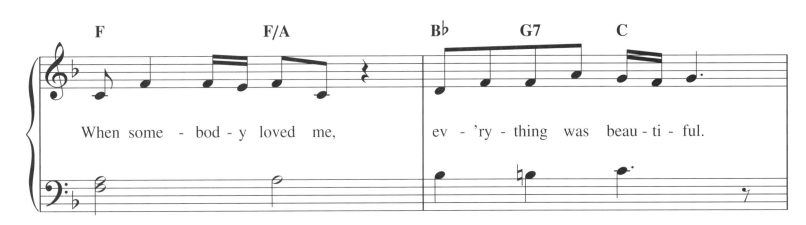

When some - bod - y loved me, ev - 'ry - thing was beau - ti - ful.

Ev - 'ry hour we spent to - geth - er lives with - in my heart, when

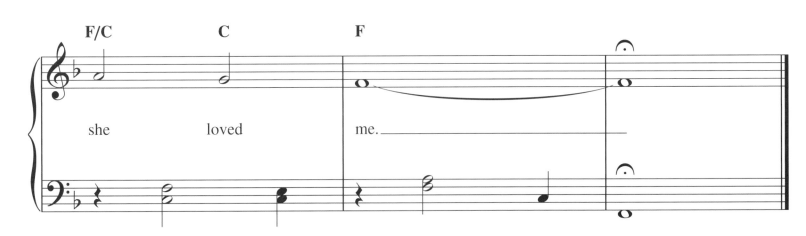

she loved me.

A WHOLE NEW WORLD

from Walt Disney's ALADDIN

Music by ALAN MENKEN
Lyrics by TIM RICE

Slowly and sweetly

With pedal

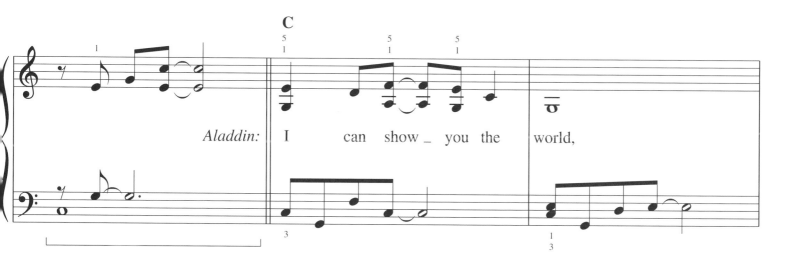

Aladdin: I can show you the world,

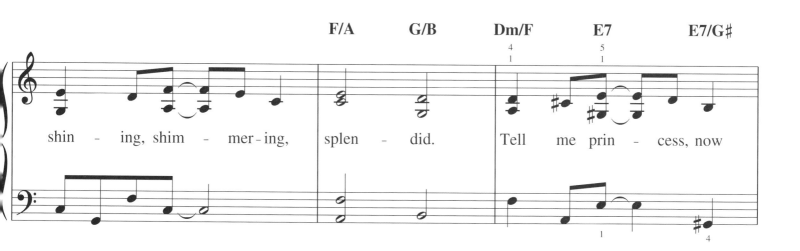

shin - ing, shim - mer - ing, splen - did. Tell me prin - cess, now

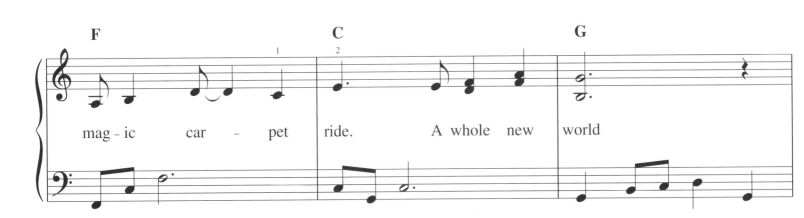

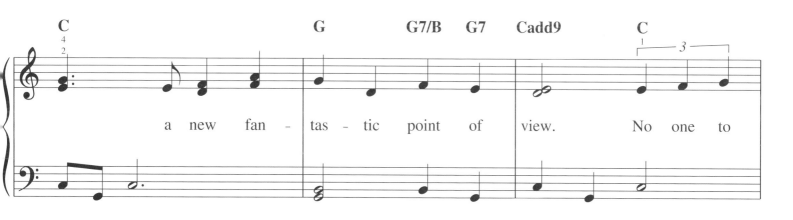

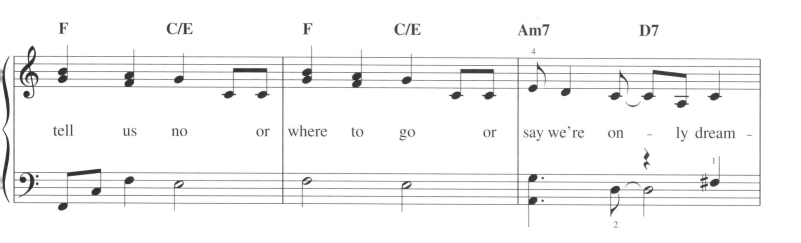

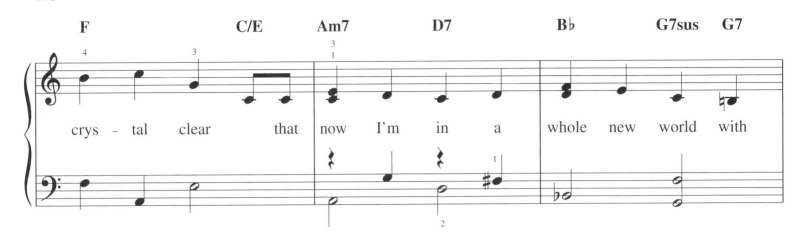

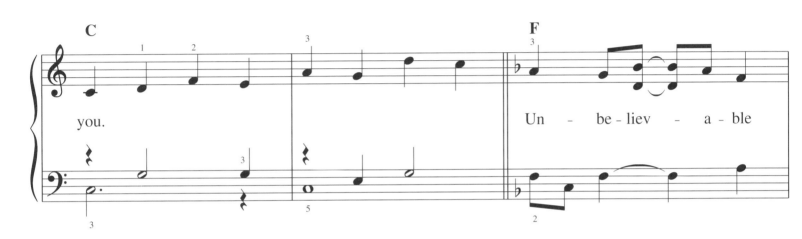

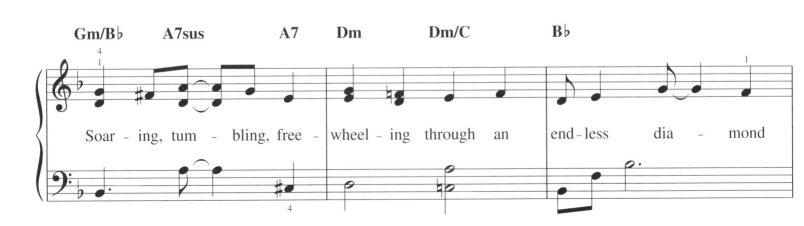

YOU ARE THE MUSIC IN ME

from the Disney Channel Original Movie HIGH SCHOOL MUSICAL 2

Words and Music by
JAMIE HOUSTON

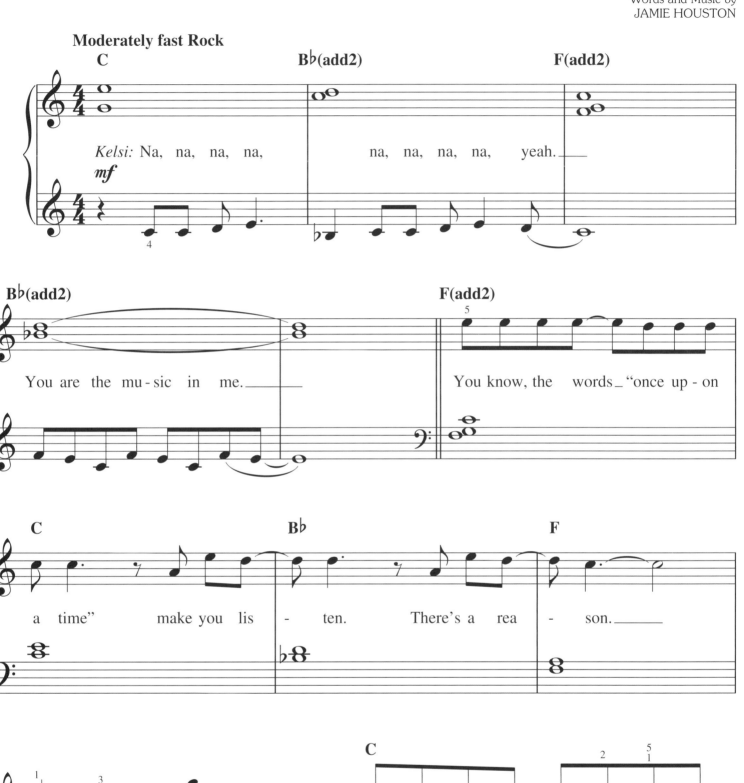

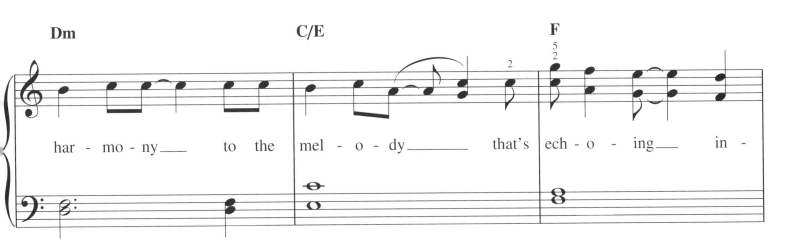

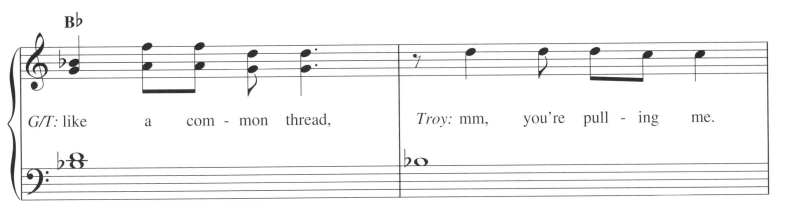

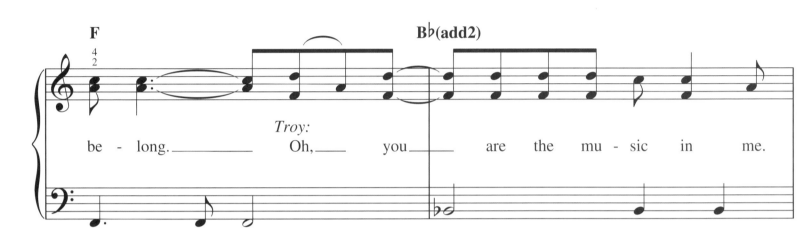

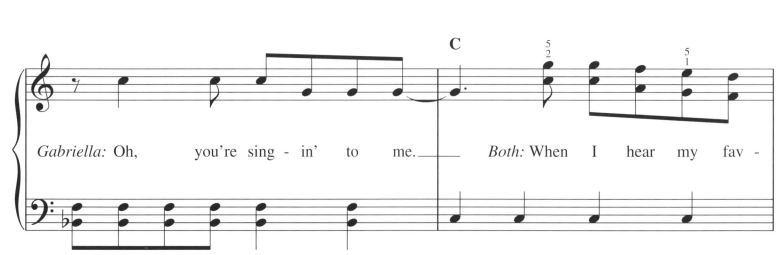

'rite song, I know that we be-long. You___ are the mu-sic in me.___

___ It's liv-in' in all of us, and it's brought us here be-cause

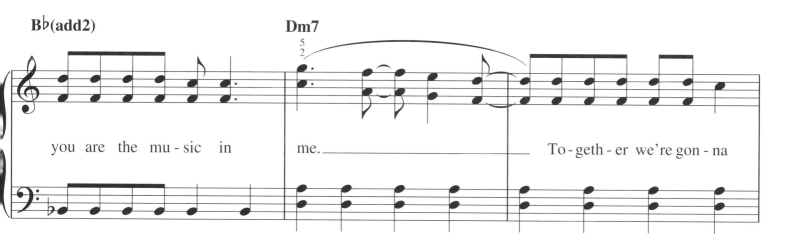

you are the mu-sic in me._____ To-geth-er we're gon-na

sing._____ We got the pow-er to say what we feel,___ con-

Troy:

258

nect-ed and real,___ *Gabriella:* can't keep it all___ in-side.

C   **B♭6**   **F**

All: (Na, na, na, na.)   (Na, na, na, na, na.)   (Na, na, na, na. You___

B♭   **C**   **B♭6**

___ are the mu-sic in me.)___   (Na, na, na, na.)   (Na, na, na, na, na.)

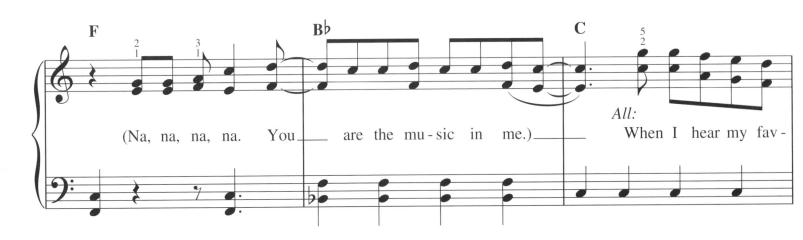

F   **B♭**   **C**

(Na, na, na, na. You___ are the mu-sic in me.)___   *All:* When I hear my fav-

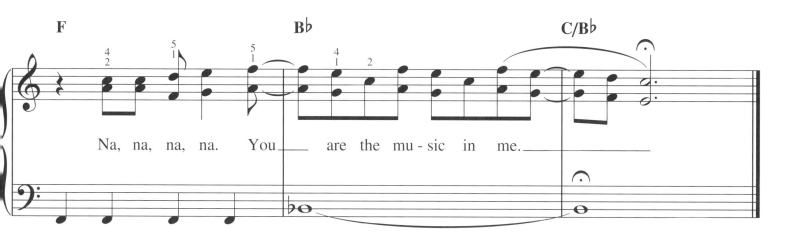

YOU'VE GOT A FRIEND IN ME

from Walt Disney's TOY STORY

Music and Lyrics by
RANDY NEWMAN

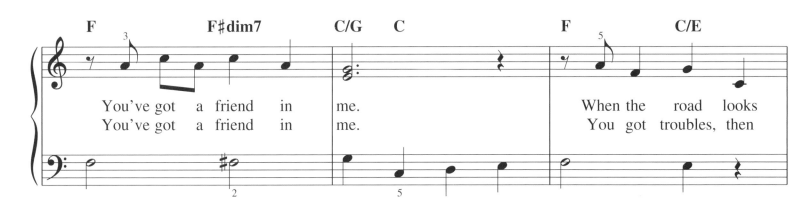

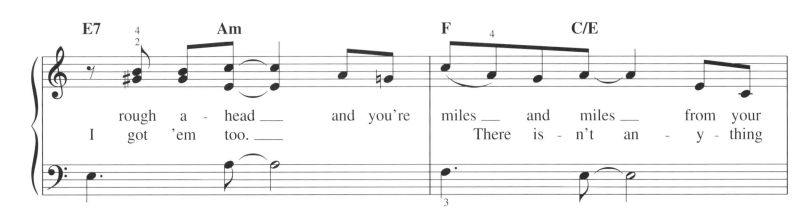

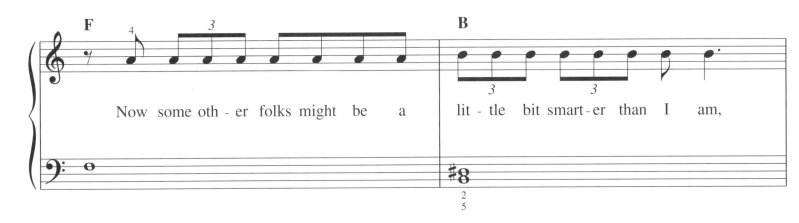

Now some oth-er folks might be a lit-tle bit smart-er than I am,

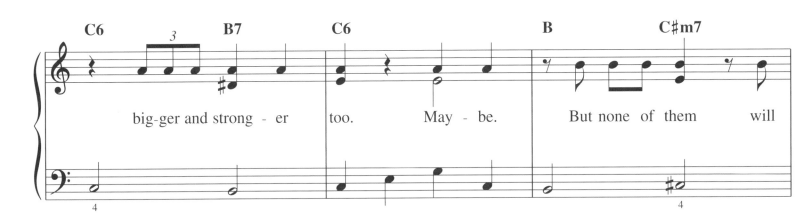

big-ger and strong - er too. May - be. But none of them will

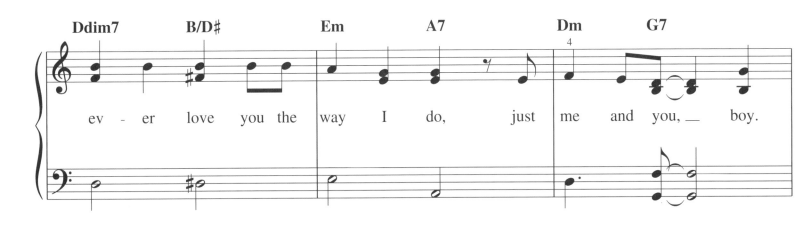

ev - er love you the way I do, just me and you, __ boy.

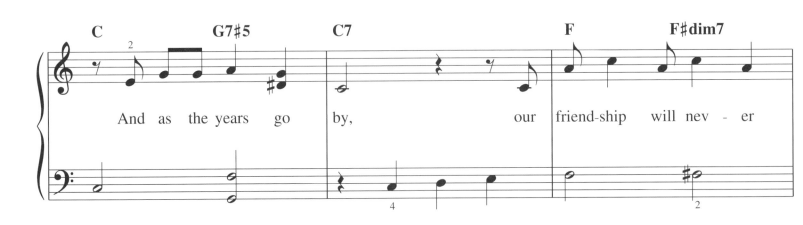

And as the years go by, our friend-ship will nev - er

ZERO TO HERO

from Walt Disney Pictures' HERCULES

Music by ALAN MENKEN
Lyrics by DAVID ZIPPEL

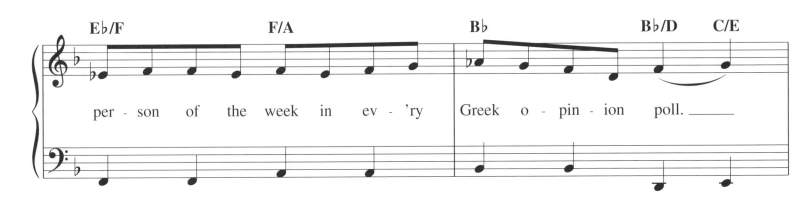

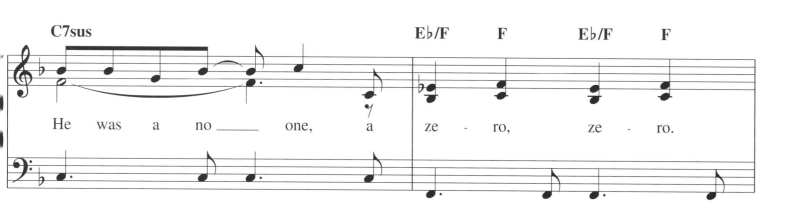

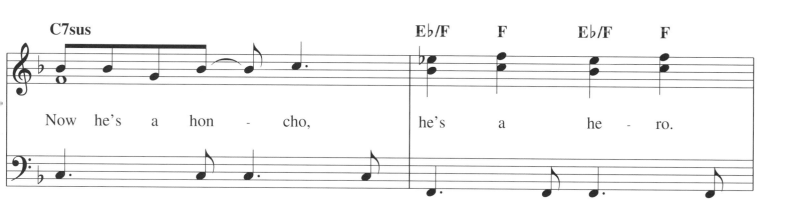

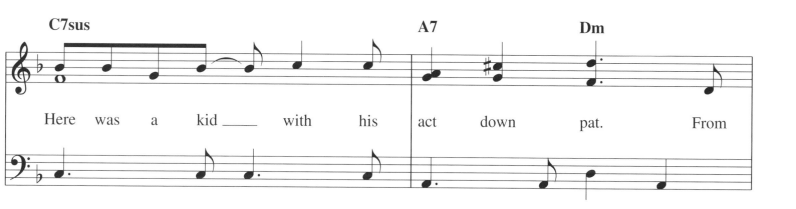

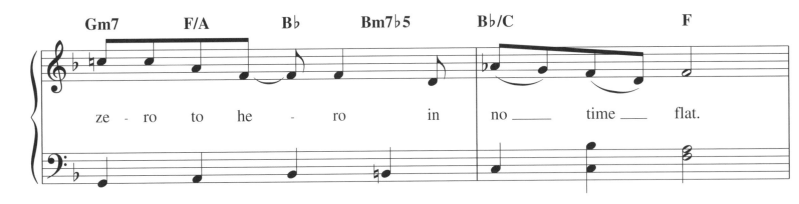

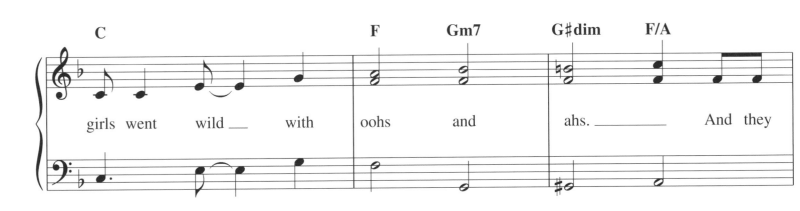

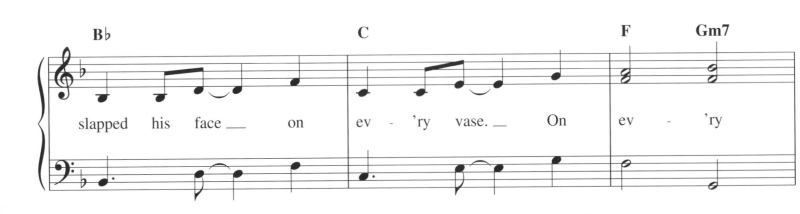

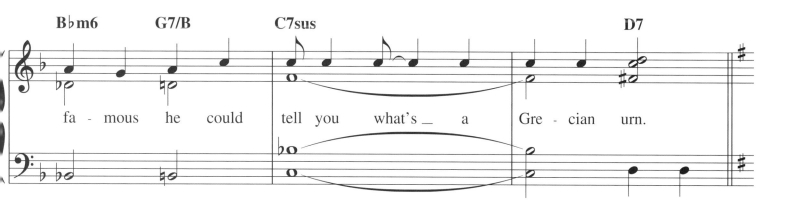

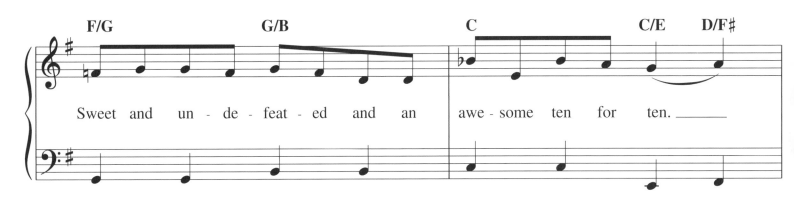

Sweet and un-de-feat-ed and an awe-some ten for ten.

Folks lined up just to watch him flex,

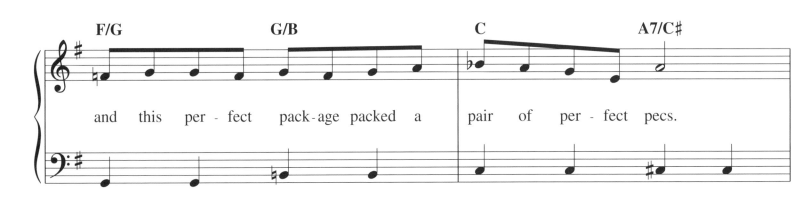

and this per-fect pack-age packed a pair of per-fect pecs.

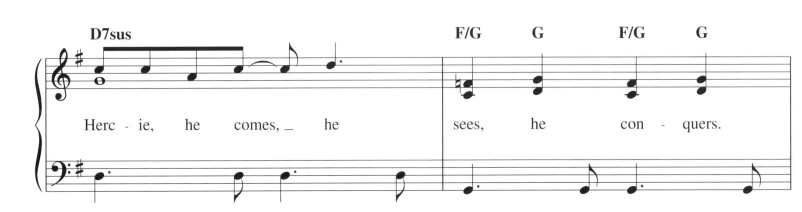

Herc - ie, he comes, _ he sees, he con - quers.

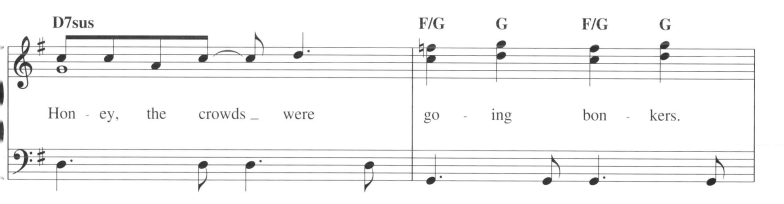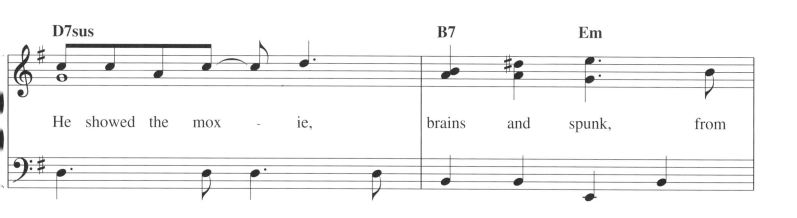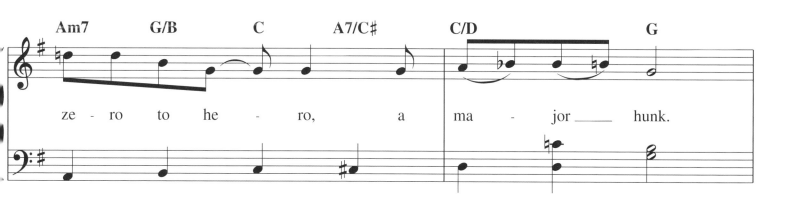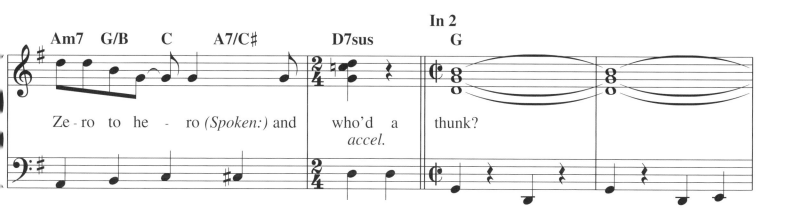

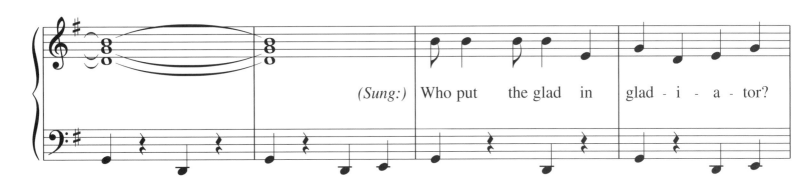

(Sung:) Who put the glad in glad - i - a - tor?

Her - cu - les. Whose dar-ing deeds _ are great the - a - ter?

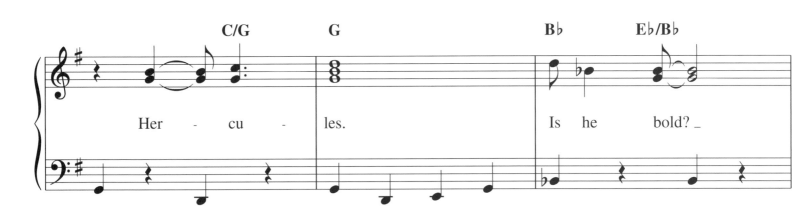

Her - cu - les. Is he bold? _

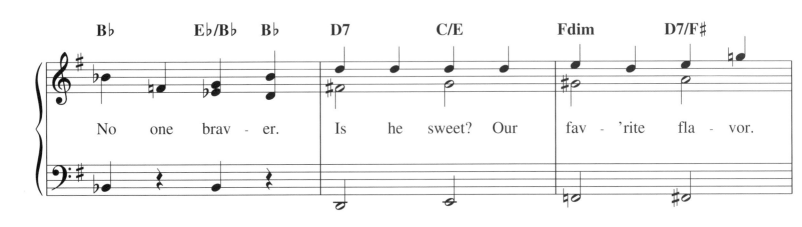

No one brav - er. Is he sweet? Our fav - 'rite fla - vor.

Her - cu - les.
Her - cu - les.

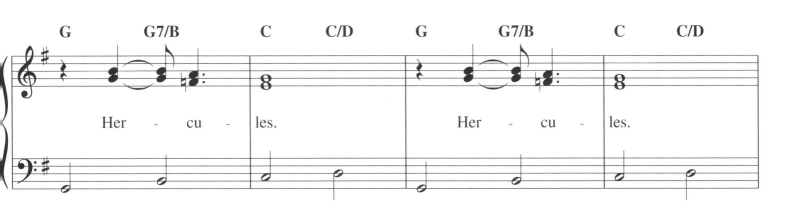

Her - cu - les.
Her - cu - les.

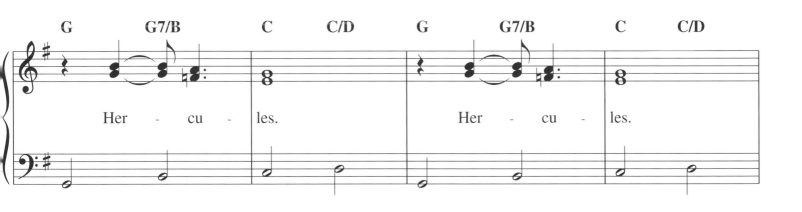

Her - cu - les.
Her - cu - les.

Bless my soul, Herc was on a roll, un - de -

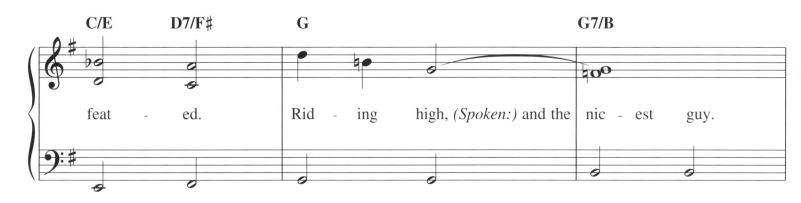

feat - ed. Rid - ing high, *(Spoken:)* and the nic - est guy.

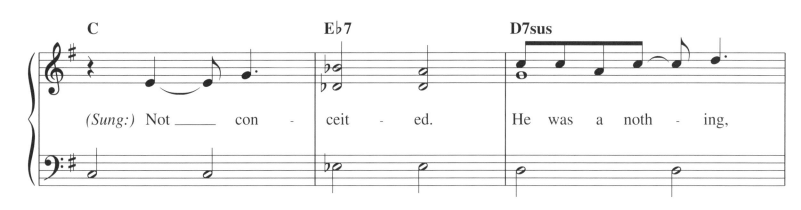

(Sung:) Not _____ con - ceit - ed. He was a noth - ing,

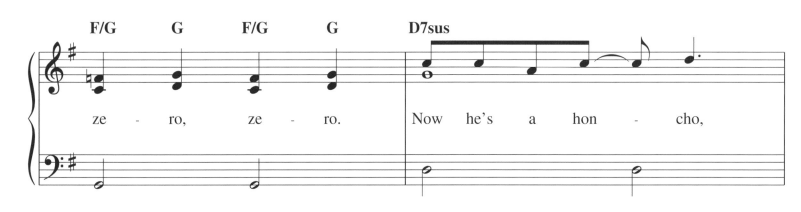

ze - ro, ze - ro. Now he's a hon - cho,

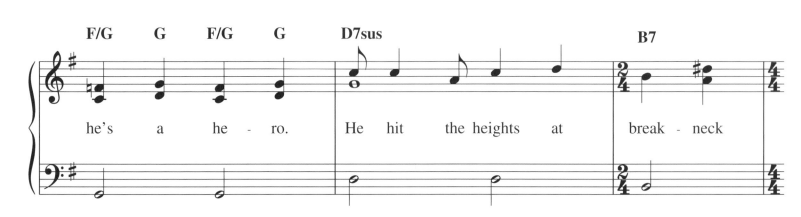

he's a he - ro. He hit the heights at break - neck

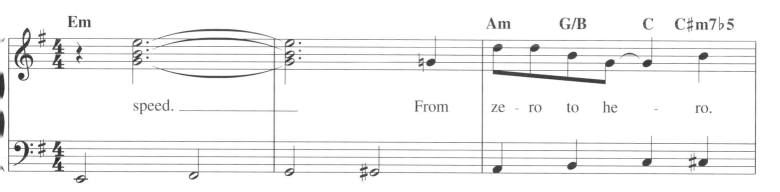

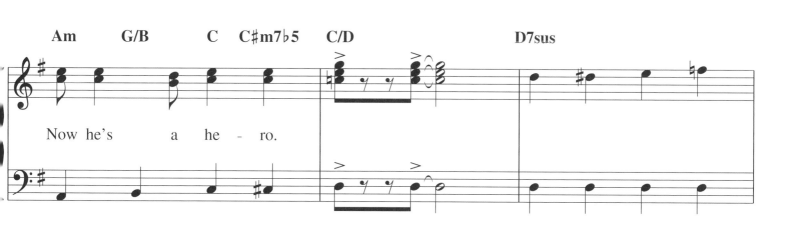

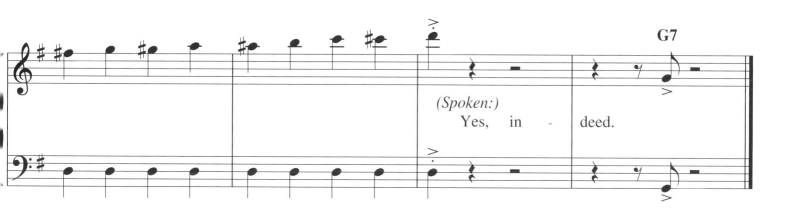

YOU'LL BE IN MY HEART

(Pop Version)
from Walt Disney Pictures' TARZAN™

Words and Music by
PHIL COLLINS

Moderately

simile

Come stop your cry-ing; it will be all right. —

Just take my hand,   hold   it   tight. —   I will pro-tect you   from

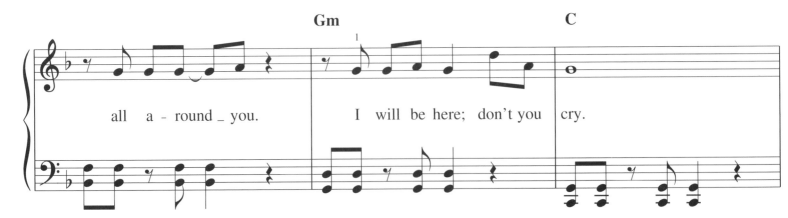

all   a - round — you.   I will be here; don't you cry.